feng shui

SECRETS
THAT CHANGE
YOUR LIFE

LI PAK TIN *&* HELEN YEAP

SAMUEL WEISER, INC.
York Beach, Maine

First published in 1997 by
SAMUEL WEISER, INC.
Box 612
York Beach, ME 03910-0612

Library of Congress Cataloging-in-Publication Data

Li, Pak Tin.
    Feng Shui : secrets that change your life / Li Pak
Tin, Helen Yeap.
        p.   cm.
    Includes index.
    ISBN 1-57863-005-3 (pbk. : alk. paper)
    1. Feng-shui. I. Yeap, Helen. II. Title.
BF1779.F4L49   1997
133.3'337--dc21   96-53234
                                                        CIP

ISBN 1-57863-005-3
BJ

Typeset in 11 point Hiroshige Book
Cover and text design by Kathryn Sky-Peck

Printed in the United States of America

03 02 01 00
10 9 8 7 6 5 4 3

Table of Contents

CHAPTER 1

What is Feng Shui?

FENG SHUI is the ancient Chinese art of placement in relation to energy. With the motion of Earth, astral and magnetic influences vary, affecting people to different degrees. Feng Shui is about fine-tuning your physical surroundings to harmonize with your inner Ch'i (life force), based upon the premise that an imbalance of energies displaces good luck and brings about internal disorders.

An understanding and recognition of the positive features that enhance the free flow of energy will make a direct impact on your well-being and financial prosperity, both at home and at work.

You all know that there are "hot" and "cold" spots in a house. The purpose of having a house Feng Shui-ed is to enable you to locate the best spot, for example, to place your desk or office when you might otherwise have allocated that area as a second bathroom. Moreover, you may wish to have your bed or sofa moved away from a "cold" spot and replace it with some heavy ornament, in order to confine the adverse energies to that place and not leave them to circulate about the rest of the house.

Being able to change the energy around you is just a part of the many balancing and compensating uses of Feng Shui—namely the symbolic unblocking of energy meridians through the staying, removing, and counterbalancing of obstacles.

Ch'i is the animating life force that is everywhere; it permeates your home, physical surroundings, the rivers, roads, trees, and all people. The purpose of Feng Shui, the "art of placement," is to enable you to tap beneficial Ch'i energy to the maximum, in order to disperse, disrupt, or remove obstructions to the free flow of Ch'i.

There are many manifestations of just how dark and dismal life can get on the wrong side of Feng Shui. Fortunately, there are corrective measures—and Feng Shui experts can make appropriate calculations that strike the desired compromises based on your date of birth and the corresponding energy meridian.

People are buying new homes as they get more secure, or as they move from one job to another. It's important that these homes harmonize with the living land, and be positioned in such a way that they are poised to ride the winds of prosperity, health, and longevity. To this end we will begin with a positive, practical analysis on harmony and Ch'i (life-breath), using Feng Shui.

While many people may be interested in using Feng Shui to buy homes and to rearrange living space for maximum good energy, the text can also be used by apartment dwellers. The main entrance to the apartment building, and the placement of the building in the community, will be read in the same way as you would read the text to determine how your house stands on the land.

The two most important things to think about are the shape and the layout of the house, itself, the direction of the front door, the direction of the bedroom door, and the placement of your bed within the structure. You can learn about your personal year, and how to use this energy for maximum benefit. The best placement of objects in the house, the best layout for the kitchen, for example, is also discussed. You are shown how to compromise, in order to create the most suitable circumstances for all members of the family living in the house. These aspects of Feng Shui shall be discussed in the following chapters. The most important thing to understand is that Feng Shui can be used to change your circumstances, for you can alter energy, and deflect energy so that the Ch'i works in your best interests.

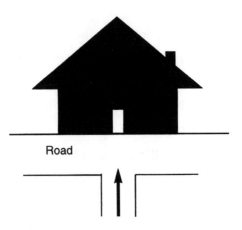

Road

EXAMPLE 1. THE T-JUNCTION HOUSE.

Situation:

When a house faces a T-junction (an allusion to a gun being pointed at it), the occupants suffer poor health and are accident prone.

Correction:

Reposition the front door so that it opens away from or at an angle to the road running up to it. Alternatively, introduce a low hedge or gate as a buffer.

FIGURE 1. THE HOUSE AT THE T-JUNCTION AT
THE END OF THE BLOCK.

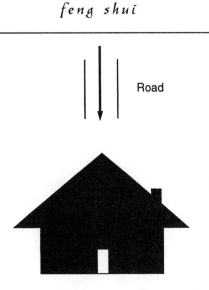

EXAMPLE 2. THE BACK-STABBING HOUSE.

Situation:

When a house has a road running toward the back (back-stabbing) there will be a lot of petty talk behind your back. Promotion prospects on your job will be bleak, even though you may be diligent and hard-working.

Correction:

Use a mirror, placed on a wall, gate, or hedge at the back of the house, where it will catch the image of the road running up to it.

CHAPTER 2

Houses in Relation to Roads

Situation:

When the road "hits" the house at an angle, money drains away. If coming from the right-hand side (A), female occupants are accident-prone. If from the left-hand side (B), male occupants are accident-prone. See example 3.

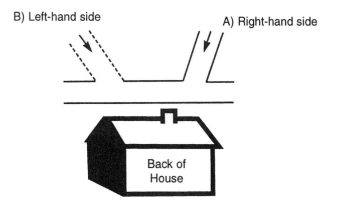

B) Left-hand side   A) Right-hand side

Back of House

EXAMPLE 3. THE ROAD HITS THE HOUSE.

Correction:

Reposition the front door so that it opens away from or at an angle to the road running up to it. Alternatively, introduce a low hedge or gate as a buffer.

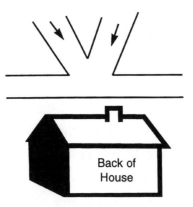

EXAMPLE 4. THE HOUSE LACKS HEALTH.

Situation:

When the road angles directly at the house, as shown in example 4 on page 8, both male and female occupants suffer poor health. In addition, they constantly bicker over financial matters.

Correction:

Reposition the front door so that it opens away from or at an angle to the road running up to it. Alternatively, introduce a low hedge or gate as a buffer.

•••

Ch'i energy is positive when, like a ventilating breeze, it is allowed to travel freely, lightly brushing everything it touches. Ch'i becomes negative energy when allowed to stagnate in dark nooks and crannies. It is positively harmful when channeled too quickly along straight paths, like a thunderbolt being hurled at your home.

With this image in mind, it follows that examples 1 through 4 (pages 4, 6, 7, 8) require an effective (albeit symbolic) buffer, such as:

A. A round convex mirror affixed above the front door to deflect negative energy;
B. A low hedge or gate introduced as buffer;
C. The front door repositioned in such a way that it opens away from, or at an angle to, the road running up to it.

Apply whichever of these remedial measures seems more appropriate in your particular circumstance.

By the same reasoning, these buffers would also apply to examples 5, 6, and 7 on pages 10 and 11.

"Scissors"
effect
intersection.

Situation:

When a house faces a crossroads (marked "X") or is located where the road forks, there will be an increased likelihood of accidents.

EXAMPLE 5. THE SCISSORS EFFECT.

Correction:

Reposition the front door so that it opens away from or at an angle to the road running up to it. Alternatively, introduce a low hedge or gate as a buffer.

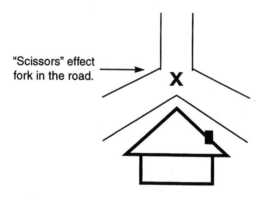

"Scissors" effect fork in the road.

EXAMPLE 6. ANOTHER KIND OF SCISSORS EFFECT.

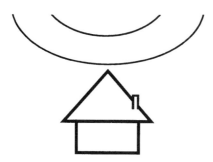

EXAMPLE 7. THE "DIP" IN THE CRESCENT.

Situation:

When a house is positioned on the convex side of a crescent, the occupants will experience financial instability, fortunes that continually rise and fall, and also a tendency to cut themselves.

Correction:

Introduce a low bush or gate between the front door and apex of the curve.

FIGURE 2. THE HOUSE ON THE CONVEX SIDE OF A CRESCENT.

Elevated highway

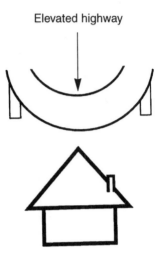

EXAMPLE 8. FINANCIAL INSTABILITY AND AN ELEVATED HIGHWAY.

Situation:

A house on this side of a crescent, having bedrooms on the same level as an elevated highway, will experience the same problems as those in example 7— only worse.

Correction:

Place convex mirror on the exterior wall.

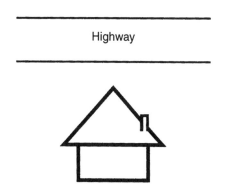

EXAMPLE 9. FACING A HIGHWAY.

Situation:

When a house is positioned alongside or facing a busy, fast-moving highway, money runs away and the occupants are unable to save money.

Correction:

Change the position of the front door. Move it to the side of the house if possible.

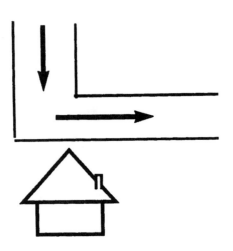

EXAMPLE 10.THE L-SHAPED ROAD

Situation:

When a house is positioned squarely at a right-angle to an L-shaped road (an allusion to a knife), it cuts both luck and money. The occupants are also accident-prone.

Correction:

If you can move the front door to the side of the house, do it. If you can't, then plant a hedge or put in a gate to make a barrier to block the "knife." You can also put a mirror over the door or raise the threshold by one inch.

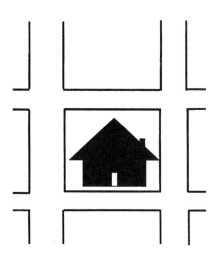

EXAMPLE 11. ONE BUILDING ON A BLOCK.

Situation:

When a single house, or an apartment house is located on a single block, and has a crossroads at each corner (as shown in example 11), it denotes that money flows out in different directions. The occupants are unable to save money.

Correction:

Raise the threshold by 1 inch.

EXAMPLE 12. THE "S" CURVE.

Situation:

When a house is in close proximity to an "S" curve, occupants enjoy prosperity. This location signifies great financial prospects.

Correction:

None necessary.

Situation:

Occupants of houses marked "X" located on this side of a road forming a semi-circle (as shown in example 13 on page 17) will reap great financial gain. The best location is at the apex of the curve.

Correction:

None necessary.

EXAMPLE 13. THE HOUSE INSIDE
THE SEMI-CIRCLE.

FIGURE 3. THE HOUSE ON A CURVE.

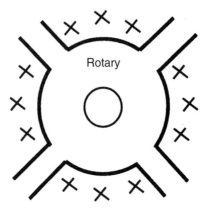

EXAMPLE 14. HOUSES AROUND A TRAFFIC CIRCLE.

FIGURE 4. A TRAFFIC CIRCLE OR ROUNDABOUT.

Situation:

Houses located near the junction ("X") of a rotary, or roundabout (as shown in example 14), are well-positioned. The location alludes to an uninterrupted flow of water, hence money comes easily.

Correction:

No correction necessary.

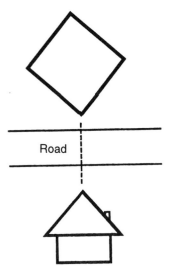

Situation:

If a corner of the house opposite points directly at a bedroom window (shown in example 15), occupants of that bedroom will suffer ill health.

EXAMPLE 15. THE BEDROOM AND THE NEIGHBORING HOUSE.

Correction:

Keep the curtains drawn in that room.

EXAMPLE 16. THE NEIGHBOR'S WINDOW.

Situation:

If a large window from the house directly opposite casts a reflection from sun upon your house (see example 16), your family will become bad-tempered and argumentative.

Correction:

Keep the curtains drawn in that room.

Situation:

Occupants of a house directly facing a gap or alley between two houses opposite (example 17) are accident-prone, constantly weak, and in poor health.

Gap

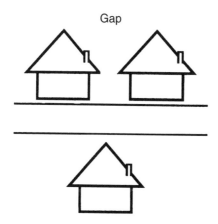

EXAMPLE 17. WHEN YOUR HOUSE FACES A GAP OR AN ALLEY.

This energy is negative only if the gap (or space) between the two houses opposite is both narrow and deep, as in figure 5.

Correction:
Deflect, using a round convex mirror, and/or raise the threshold by 2 inches.

FIGURE 5. ANOTHER EXAMPLE OF A GAP OR AN ALLEY.

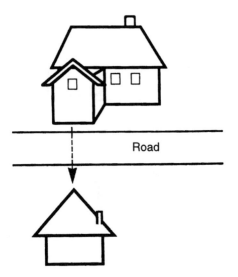

EXAMPLE 18. A WING OR EXTENSION.

Situation:

If a wing or an extension on a building or house opposite points directly at your house as shown in example 18, someone in your family may suffer heart problems.

Correction:

Place gold-colored coins under the threshold of the main door.

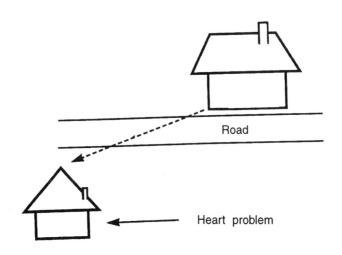

EXAMPLE 19. ANGULAR CORNERS.

Situation:

Similarly, if a corner of the house opposite is aimed at your house, someone in the family may suffer from heart problems.

Correction:

Deflect the energy, using a round convex mirror.

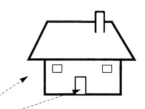

EXAMPLE 20. A TRIANGULAR
FEATURE.

Situation:

If a triangular feature on the house opposite yours faces your front door or bedroom window, the occupants of that bedroom, or occupants of your house, will be accident-prone.

Correction:

Hang net curtains in the affected bedroom.

FIGURE 6. A TURRET OR TOWER WITH TRIANGULAR ENERGY.

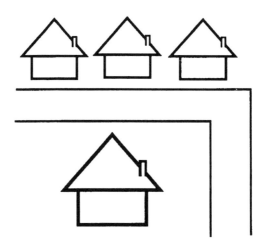

EXAMPLE 21. THE INVERTED L-SHAPE.

Situation:

Occupants of houses directly opposite an inverted L-shaped road frequently encounter people overwhelmed with petty problems.

Correction:

If you live in any one of these houses, hang a convex mirror on the door, or raise the threshold slightly.

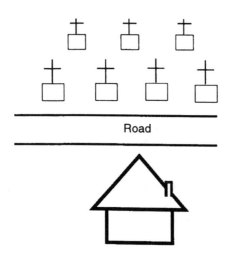

Road

EXAMPLE 22. THE HOUSE ACROSS FROM A CEMETERY,
HOSPITAL, OR FUNERAL HOME.

Situation:

Occupants of houses opposite a cemetery, hospital, or funeral parlor will be dogged by a series of unspecified illnesses, and are often susceptible to nightmares.

Correction:

Leave one light switched on both night and day.

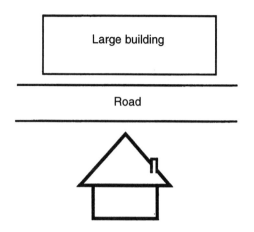

EXAMPLE 23. THE HOUSE ACROSS
FROM A VERY LARGE BUILDING.

Situation:

Occupants of a house opposite a very large building often fall victim to fraud.

Correction:

Do not lend money to anyone if you live in such a location.

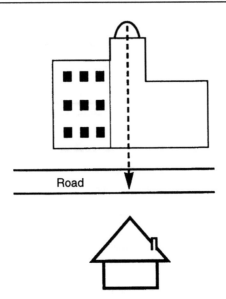

EXAMPLE 24. THE HOUSE ACROSS FROM A DOME.

Situation:

The children who live in houses facing a round feature or dome (must be directly opposite) will have behavioral problems. Ensure that the children's bedrooms do not look out over the dome.

Correction:

You could swap bedrooms with the children, as dome features do not affect adults.

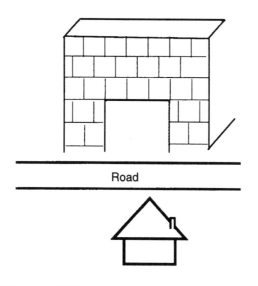

EXAMPLE 25. THE HOUSE ACROSS FROM A GATEWAY
INTO AN ALLEY.

Situation:

When a house directly faces a gateway into an alley or courtyard, the occupants will suffer poor health and will be unable to achieve their full potential at work.

Correction:

Change the position of the front door so that it does not open opposite the gateway.

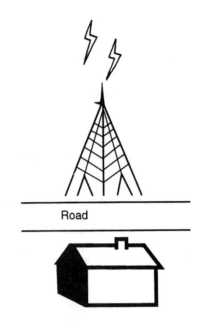

EXAMPLE 26. HOUSES OPPOSITE ELECTRICAL PYLONS.

Situation:

When a house is immediately opposite an electric pylon (a major power source), the occupants will be susceptible to illness. The house is prone to fire of various kinds.

Correction:

Deflect the energy by placing an octagonal mirror above the front door.

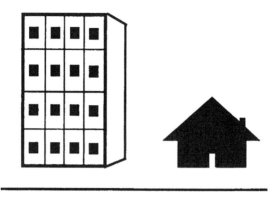

EXAMPLE 27. A HOUSE NEXT TO A TALL BUILDING.

Situation:

A large, tall building to the right side of your house (as shown in example 27) will cause the occupants to constantly argue among themselves.

Correction:

Place a free-hanging piece of crystal on the bedroom window to project dancing dots of sunlight onto the bedroom walls.

EXAMPLE 28. THE HOUSE IN A GOOD LOCATION.

Situation:

If the house is flanked on either side by a house of similar size, or a taller or detached house, then help is always close at hand.

Correction:

None necessary for this beneficial placement.

Situation:

A church directly opposite a house renders the occupants quick-tempered and very lonely.

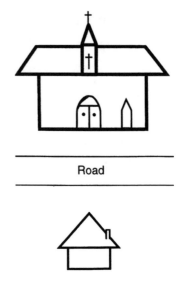

Road

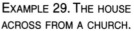

Correction: Place a convex mirror on the door to deflect the energy. Occupants will not be affected if the church stands 100 feet away.

EXAMPLE 29. THE HOUSE ACROSS FROM A CHURCH.

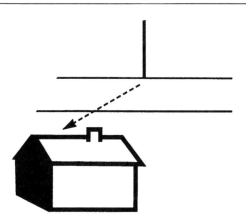

EXAMPLE 30. THE HOUSE AT AN ANGLE TO A LAMPPOST.

Situation:

A lamppost directly in line with the front door leads to litigation and ill health.

Correction:

Deflect the energy by placing a convex mirror over the door.

FIGURE 7. NOTE THE LAMP-POST AT AN ANGLE TO THE FRONT DOOR.

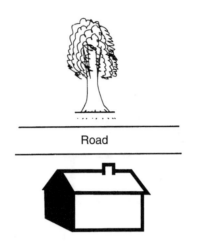

EXAMPLE 31. A TREE OPPOSITE THE FRONT DOOR.

Situation:

And similarly with a tree opposite that is directly in line with the front door.

Correction:

Deflect the energy by placing a round convex mirror over the door.

FIGURE 8. PLACE A MIRROR ON THE DOOR TO DEFLECT THE TREE.

•••

Note that the purpose of these corrective measures is either to increase receptivity, to focus and channel positive energy, or conversely, to deflect negative influences.

Obstacles to the front door—a chimney, lamppost, pylon, cemetery, etc.—positioned 100 feet away from the door no longer affect the house. The influence of these external features is greatest when they are directly in line with the main door. (See figure 9 for

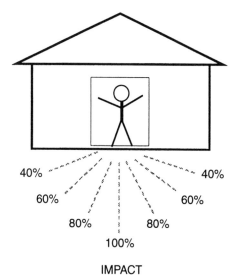

IMPACT

FIGURE 9. ANGULAR STRENGTH OF AN OBSTACLE. NOTE THAT YOU ARE ALWAYS STANDING INSIDE YOUR HOUSE LOOKING OUT WHEN YOU DETERMINE DIRECTION.

an idea of the anglar strength of something you are trying to avoid.) The impact of these obstacles is lessened
the more the obstacle is angled away from the main
door. This is one reason why it helps when doors are
repositioned at a slight angle, away from the direct
path of an obstacle.

CHAPTER 3

Buying a House

UNLESS YOUR birthdate is compatible with the WAN (see page 55) of the potential purchase and accords favorably with the aspect of the house, it's best to avoid houses in the categories discussed in the following text. Alternatively, you could enlist the balancing skill of a Feng Shui expert to offset the shortcomings that we mention here.

When buying a house, ascertain the reason for the sale. Find out if the previous owner experienced a sudden bankruptcy. Bankruptcy is only acceptable when it is attributable to a general economic depression.

If you are looking at a vacant house, ascertain why it is vacant. If the owners have passed on due to old age, that would be considered a natural occurrence. If, however, a previous occupant died in an accident, or before age 40, it is best to avoid it, lest you take on their misfortune.

If the house has experienced a fire more than once, this is a strong indication that it is a fire-prone plot.

Large underground water pipes laid in a back to front direction, and running just under the main door, symbolize a constant drain of financial resources away from the house.

Properties above underground tunnels are best avoided, as the intermittent "chopping" vibrations coming from beneath symbolize a general undermining of all efforts.

HOUSE SHAPES

Houses correspond directly to the five elements. For instance, a house that has a circular or crescent-shaped floorplan is termed a METAL house; a long or L-shaped house is a WOOD house; a house located on a triangular plot is a FIRE house; a square-ish floorplan is an EARTH house; a house having numerous bays is a WATER house.

The choice of a METAL house (circular or crescent-shaped) is ideal for those who dabble in the stock market and who are commercially minded. The rise in good fortune will be speedy while the cyclical twenty-year span of prosperity lasts, after which there will be a marked downward trend.

A WATER house (with numerous bays) is like the ebb and flow of the tide, and experiences quick changes in fortunes. The watery inconsistency offers no promises of financial security.

With a FIRE house (built on a triangular plot), as the flames of a fire leap up and down, so both the health and the financial situation of a family will fluctuate.

The best houses are those belonging to the stoic WOOD and EARTH types.

YIN AND YANG

These are the polar opposites of all existence. YANG represents the vigorous, pulsating energy of the Dragon. YIN symbolizes the calm stillness of the sleeping Tiger. YIN and YANG are complementary forces which continually interact, creating change. See Table 1 on page 40.

Where they blend to achieve the appropriate balance, there is harmony. For example, an introduction of shrubs, rose arches, and rock gardens can have a pleasing effect on a flat landscape.

Table 1. YIN and YANG for Feng Shui.

Yang Elements	Yin Elements
People	Houses
Animals	Forest, trees, small hills
Light	Dark
Artificial lighting	Inanimate objects

If, before entering a house, you sense "darkness" that is attributable to dense foliage, wildly overgrown hedges, or a house in too close proximity to woodlands, you will know that the light of YANG is being stifled. In Feng Shui, it is said that if the Sun does not visit your house, the doctor will.

Generally, the more windows there are in a house, the better. Happily, you can always introduce instant solutions, such as picture windows, portholes, etc. However, if there are too many windows, this may also mean that you are mixing air from different directions. Keep some windows shut.

A window looking out to a round satellite dish detracts energy from the house. To correct this, place plants on the window sill, or introduce curtains, but you need not keep the curtains drawn.

Windows facing somebody else's garden or look-ing at a neighbor's clothesline, especially with lots of ladies underclothes hanging on the line, give too much YIN. To deflect this energy, put curtains on either side of that window (you needn't keep them drawn). If the clothesline is 100 feet away, then it does not affect the house. However, if you buy a house that looks over a clothesline, you may want to avoid gambling.

CHAPTER 4

Physical Features Affecting Feng Shui

F ENG S HUI simply means "mountain water." Mountains offer a vantage position plus shelter from harsh winds, while water nurtures the soil. For the ancient Chinese, mountains control people, water dictates the flow of money. The site chosen to build a home would, of necessity, have the presence of both a mountain and water. Traditionally, the ancient Chinese would decline to build a home where either of these qualities is absent.

Land features, such as rivers and mountains, are of great significance, either in themselves, or in symbolized form. For example, mountains are represented by tall buildings, rivers by roads.

MOUNTAIN

In Feng Shui terminology, "mountain" refers to large edifices within the immediate surroundings of a house. Mountains play a vital role in that they symbolize support and positions of command. To realize this supportive potential, it follows that such a building should be higher and larger than your house. The power derived from having such support is as follows:

- People do things for you;

- They receive and accept your ideas readily;

- They are able and willing to care for you.

A mountain behind a house indicates that the inhabitants will inherit wealth. A solitary house (i.e., houses to its left and right being some distance away) is without left or right "helpers." Thus the occupants must learn to be self-reliant.

How do you define a "good" mountain? Figure 10 shows how the mountain corresponds to the five elements.

Note that the summit of mountains must not be crowned with rocks. Buildings cannot be jagged against the skyline (e.g., adorned with aerials, lighted neon signs, etc.) To correct such a situation, hang net curtains to obscure these from view. Alternatively, deflect by placing a round convex mirror on the exterior wall to neutralize negative features.

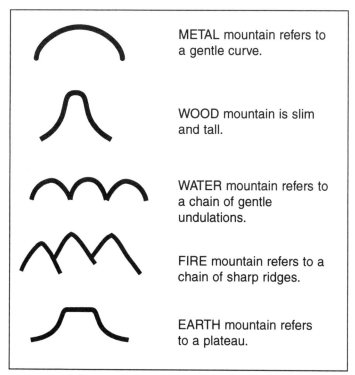

METAL mountain refers to a gentle curve.

WOOD mountain is slim and tall.

WATER mountain refers to a chain of gentle undulations.

FIRE mountain refers to a chain of sharp ridges.

EARTH mountain refers to a plateau.

FIGURE 10. THE MOUNTAIN AND THE ELEMENTS. THESE SHAPES PORTEND GOOD LUCK EXCEPT FOR THE FIRE MOUNTAIN.

Situation:

Rocky or jagged mountain tops and skylines behind a house will mean that people will constantly talk behind your back. You will make enemies, and those in high positions will argue with you. The family is prone to skin problems, stomach ailments, even measles, and something is always wrong. The occu-

EXAMPLE 32. JAGGED MOUNTAINTOPS
BEHIND THE HOUSE.

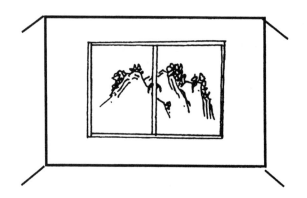

EXAMPLE 33. EYE PROBLEMS COME FROM LOOKING AT JAGGED
OR ROCKY MOUNTAINS.

pants, particularly of South-facing houses that look out directly to "bad" mountains, have a propensity to suffer from poor eyesight and eye-associated ills (examples 32, 33).

Rocky mountains behind a house will cause petty misfortunes to befall the occupants, and anyone looking out to such a mountain will be prone to eye problems.

Correction:

Hang net curtains to obscure such a view.

HOUSES TO THE LEFT OR RIGHT
OF YOUR HOME—THE DRAGON AND THE TIGER

In the absence of mountains, the houses to the left and right represent mountains by analogy. To the left, the Green Dragon, which is the masculine influence, predominates, while the White Tiger (its feminine counterpart) rules the right-hand side. To determine direction, stand in the doorway, facing the street.

If, in linked houses, or town houses, or brownstones, those to the right stand taller or closer together, or if there are more houses to the right, then the

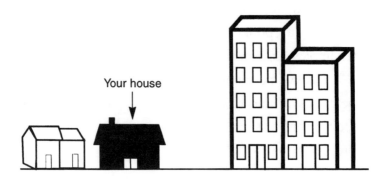

EXAMPLE 34. TIGER ON RIGHT; DRAGON ON LEFT.

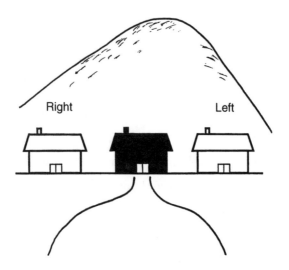

EXAMPLE 35. A GOOD HOUSE WITH A **METAL** SHAPED
MOUNTAIN AT THE BACK.

Right   Left

EXAMPLE 36. THE HOUSE WITH LITTLE GOOD FORTUNE.

White Tiger predominates (i.e., the woman of the house wields the power). And the reverse is true. Where houses on the left stand nearer, and those to the right stand farther away, the masculine influence predominates. When Dragon is higher and Tiger is lower, the man runs the house (example 34).

A "good" house will have a METAL-shaped mountain to the rear (i.e., people continually offering assistance), a Dragon to its left, and a Tiger on its right (example 35).

Right   Left

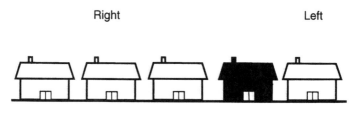

EXAMPLE 37. ANOTHER HOUSE WITH LITTLE LUCK COMING TO OCCUPANTS.

Where there is a row of three houses, and there are two Dragons to the left, but the Tiger is absent, luck comes, but in a trickle (example 36).

On the other hand, if there are two Tigers next to a row of three houses, the Tiger is stronger than the Dragon, and the occupants can expect no windfalls either. The women will enjoy more luck than the men in this house (example 37).

ROAD/MOUNTAINS

By analogy, a ground level 1 inch higher than the house represents a mountain; a ground level 1 inch lower than the house represents a road.

A house is deemed sound if the road on which it is situated is without a bend, or there is a long road opposite the house.

A generous bay or space in front of the house is conducive to the free flow of fresh air; its occupants will enjoy the comforts that make life worth living. However, meager spaces are tell-tale signs of pressured, restless, and nervous occupants.

The ideal set-up is a mountain or large house behind your house, with a generous space to the front of it (example 38).

EXAMPLE 38. TALL BUILDING (OR MOUNTAIN) BEHIND THE HOUSE.

EXAMPLE 39. TO CORRECT FOR A PARK BEHIND THE HOUSE, THE
ROAD CAN GO ACROSS THE FRONT OF THE HOUSE; OR IT CAN CURVE
SLIGHTLY, BUT IT SHOULD NOT LEAD STRAIGHT UP TO THE HOUSE (AS
IN A T-JUNCTION OR IN THE BACK-STABBING EXAMPLES).

A string of houses behind your house is still favorable by way of continual support, but occupants of houses that back onto parks and open spaces will not find support in their ventures (example 39).

Correction: Add shrubs to the garden; erect a low fence along the border of the garden.

WATER

Water is of paramount importance in the art of Feng Shui. In Feng Shui terminology, it refers to the financial situation. It is difficult in inner cities to ascertain whether or not houses look onto water. However in Feng Shui, by analogy, water refers to roads. Some people construct fountains on their property, hopeful of continuous financial gains.

There are five different types of water corresponding to the five elements. They determine the state of your finances. The flow of traffic, or passersby, or a stream in front of your house, all indicate the flow of your money. See figure 11 on page 53.

THE QUALITY OF WATER

If the flow of water or traffic on your street is clear and light, money will come to you surely, but unhurriedly.

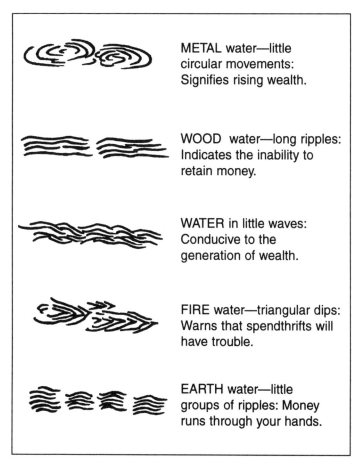

METAL water—little circular movements: Signifies rising wealth.

WOOD water—long ripples: Indicates the inability to retain money.

WATER in little waves: Conducive to the generation of wealth.

FIRE water—triangular dips: Warns that spendthrifts will have trouble.

EARTH water—little groups of ripples: Money runs through your hands.

FIGURE 11. THE FLOW OF MONEY.

A light swishing indicates that money will flow to you. If the river or road should encircle your house, there is a high propensity to make great savings. If the directional flow of water is auspicious for that twenty-year cycle, you will reap quick rewards financially.

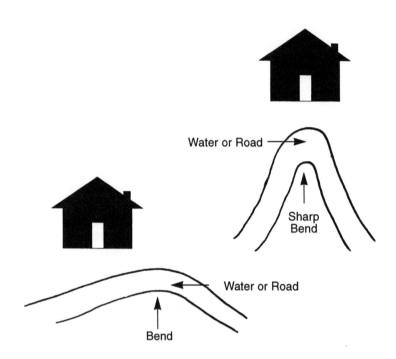

EXAMPLE 40. THE HOUSE AT THE SHARP BEND IN THE ROAD DOES
NOT BRING FINANCIAL STABILITY.

However, if water (or traffic) is polluted, you will
keep missing the correct strategies to generate wealth.
Moreover, the occupants of the house, while they find
themselves unable to keep their money, will also suffer from poor health. And worse still, houses that look
onto noisy water (or traffic) will be plagued by financial losses and family dissension.

FIGURE 12. HOUSES FACING WATER.

It is best to avoid houses situated on the crook of a pronounced bend of a riverbed or street (example 40), as that is equated with the erosion of wealth—like a weed wacker cutting away opportunities. To correct this problem, install a low gate between the front door and the road.

"TONG WAN":
THE AUSPICIOUS DIRECTION

WAN refers to the directional changes calculated within twenty-year cycles on the premise that every twenty years the "good" and "bad" positions undergo a change of direction. Thus the fortunes of a house wax and wane over a twenty-year cycle. For directional changes, refer to Table 2 on pages 57–58.

It is not true that it is always lucky to face water. Apart from the quality and general appearance of water, as previously mentioned, whether it is TONG WAN for the relevant year is also a critical factor to consider. If your house looks onto a stream, it is very important to ascertain whether the directional aspect of the water is auspicious.

According to Table 2, water to the East is TONG WAN for 1997. This means that if there is a stream or street East of your house, you will experience the "Midas touch." Conversely, if the house faces West, and looks onto water, financial losses are to be expected. This may explain your neighbor's enthusiastic commissioning of an ornamental fountain or a rockery in their front garden on a date that coincides with the threshold of the next twenty-year cycle.

If the water has the correct composition, the home owner's financial position is very strong. And even if the water is polluted or smells, provided it is TONG WAN, the financial position remains viable, but financial gains will come through dubious channels.

Table 2. Water "TONG WAN" (Auspicious Direction)

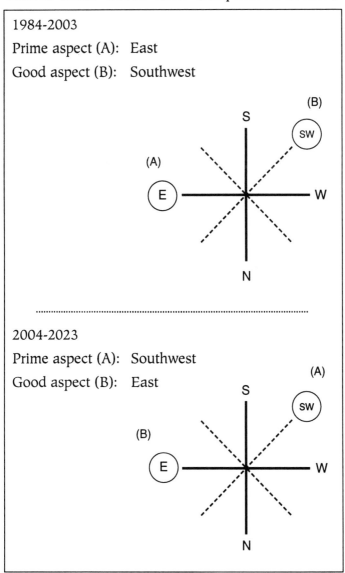

1984-2003

Prime aspect (A): East

Good aspect (B): Southwest

2004-2023

Prime aspect (A): Southwest

Good aspect (B): East

Table 2. Water "TONG WAN" (Auspicious Direction) *cont.*

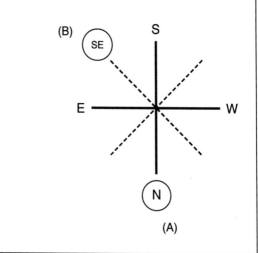

2024-2043

Prime aspect (A): North

Good aspect (B): Southeast

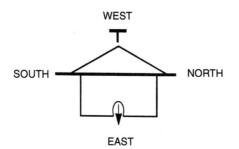

EXAMPLE 41. THE PERFECT LOCATION FOR THE TWENTY-YEAR
CYCLE FROM 1984-2003.

So if we take 1997 as an example, the prime aspect for water is East, i.e., the ideal position from 1984 to 2003 is as shown in example 41. The house should have its back to the West, its main door facing East looking onto water.

AIR

One cannot overemphasize the fundamental importance of good air, the lack of which will result in a significant reduction (up to 30 percent) in your good fortune even though you may have the advantageous presence of favorable mountains (buildings) and rivers (streets). There are three different types of air:

- WONG HEI air spells excellent wealth prospects;
- SANG HEI air is thin and diluted; hence progress comes only a step at a time;
- CHOON HEI air is ventilating, which is an improvement on SANG HEI air.

So, to determine Air in your house, find the center of the house. Never mind if that center does not allow you to see the front door. Simply stand in the central

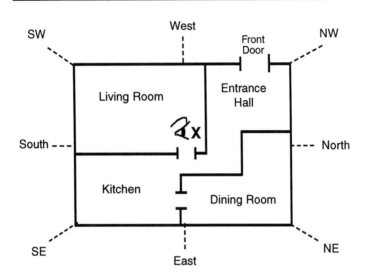

EXAMPLE 42. NOTICE THAT THE CENTER OF THE HOUSE IS
NOT VISIBLE FROM THE FRONT DOOR.

spot (marked "X" in example 42) and turn in the direction facing the front door. If your front door opens directly into the west, then you have WONG HEI air for this 7th WAN. But if, like most of us, your front door opens into another direction, the compensating Feng Shui measure is as follows. Choose as your bedroom, the room with the door opening into sections 1, 2, 3, or 4 of your relevant Personal Direction Chart. If there are no bedroom doors opening into sections 1, 2, 3, or 4 of your Personal Direction Chart, then place your bed into sections 1, 2, 3, or 4 of the room you use as your bedroom.

You will recall that TONG WAN refers to the twenty-year cycle of directional changes in energy meridian; in other words, each WAN (twenty-year time span) bears a different direction.

Check the date of your house purchase (or rental lease) against Table 3 for Air. Suppose you bought a house in 1994. Note that 1994 accords with the 7th

Table 3. Air Aspects.

YEAR	SPAN	BEST ASPECT	GOOD	FAIR
$$ PROSPECTS		WONG HEI	CHOON HEI	SANG HEI
1864-1883	1st WAN	North	Southwest	East
1884-1903	2nd WAN	Southwest	East	Southeast
1904-1923	3rd WAN	East	Southeast	CENTRAL
1924-1943	4th WAN	Southeast	CENTRAL	Northwest
1944-1963	5th WAN	CENTRAL	Northwest	West
1964-1983	6th WAN	Northwest	West	Northeast
1984-2003	7th WAN	West	Northeast	South
2004-2023	8th WAN	Northeast	South	North
2024-2043	9th WAN	South	North	Southwest

WAN in the chart, i.e., the years between 1984-2003. Therefore, the direction most conducive to Feng Shui is West; next best is North or East, and lastly, South.

With reference to Table 3, the chart for Air, if you wish to retain the property for the next forty years, it will be advantageous to purchase a house that benefits from a North or East aspect (for it then overlaps into the 8th WAN). Alternatively, you could select a South-facing direction if you wish to retain the property for the next sixty years (on the basis that the auspicious direction follows through the 8th and into the 9th WAN).

To determine the quality of air that comes in through your front door, stand in the center of your house and face the front door. The word "central" in Table 3 means that the door direction is irrelevant as long as air has easy access into the center of the house when you open the main door.

CHAPTER 5

The Front Door

THE FRONT door is associated with wealth. In Feng Shui the aspect of the main door of a house is of cardinal importance, this being the entrance that lets in or keeps out the vital energy that promotes health, luck, and wealth.

Where the house is located, and the direction it faces, are crucial considerations. The best position for the main door is in the middle of the house. With the proliferation of semi-detached and terrace-type property today, this is not generally the situation.

The air that comes in must be TONG WAN (auspicious direction). When the front door is located so that neither the Dragon nor the Tiger are able to take in air, a suffocation effect arises, and the potential for generating wealth is greatly lessened. Therefore, the positioning and aspect of the front door in relation to air is of prime importance.

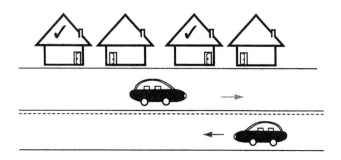

EXAMPLE 43. ENTRANCE CONFORMS TO TRAFFIC.

For the Dragon or Tiger to receive an unrestricted flow of air, it is best that the front door does not conflict with the direction of the traffic (see example 43).

A park or any similar large space at the front of the house is very good, being conducive to the free flow of air. Indeed, it makes the direction of traffic flow imma-

EXAMPLE 44. IDEALLY A PARK, LARGE SPACE, OR FOUNTAIN TO THE FRONT MAKES DIRECTION OF TRAFFIC IMMATERIAL.

terial (example 44). Provided the air is TONG WAN, even if water is absent, the house remains desirable.

What's most important is that your front door is TONG WAN, for it faces the direction most auspicious for that particular time cycle to enable it to effectively receive WANG HEI, SANG HEI, or CHOON HEI air.

From Table 3 (on page 61), you will see that 1997 lies in the 7th WAN.

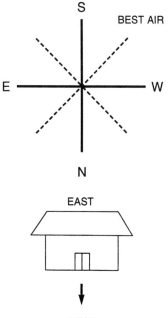

EXAMPLE 45. FOR 1984-2003 THE BEST ASPECT IS A HOUSE WITH ITS BACK TO EAST AND A FRONT DOOR THAT FACES WEST.

Provided your house faces the correct direction for the relevant time span (see Table 3, page 61), your good luck will override anything. It then becomes immaterial whether your front door is positioned in the middle of the house, or to the sides (see example 45 on page 61). Even if a house lacks water, provided it receives good air, it will basically still be a sound house.

The front door resembles the mouth of a human face, and as such has a significant overall bearing on the Feng Shui of the house. The Japanese set great store by such factors, even if intuitively. It is a known fact that part of their design research on cars focuses on the overall impact of the radiators. Market research has shown that models with radiators resembling

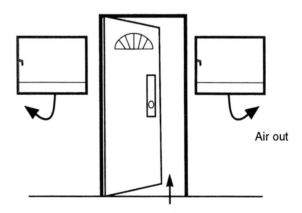

Air out

EXAMPLE 46. BENEFICIAL AIR IN.

EXAMPLE 47. PLACE PLANTS ON WINDOW SILLS.

down-turned mouths hold little appeal, being deemed "depressing."

Special emphasis is placed on the front door since all occupants pass through this entrance many times daily. Tradespeople, the postal carrier, even strangers, come to the door. If your financial situation is bad, it may also be attributed to the winds of good luck being dragged out through the windows on either side of the front door.

To correct this situation, place hardy, round-leafed plants on the window sill to keep your luck within the house.

Sometimes, particularly in large houses, there may be too many openings to contain the circulating

Ch'i (life force). It is best to leave only five doors ajar and keep the extra doors (e.g., bedrooms, bathrooms, kitchen) shut when not in use.

Symbolically speaking, bathroom air is stagnant. It is air that you don't want to have circulating around the house. If there is a bathroom directly opposite the front door, wealth is constantly being flushed away. To correct this situation, place a screen before the bathroom door so that it is not in immediate view as you enter. Use this same remedial measure when kitchen and bathroom doors are positioned exactly opposite each other. (Bathroom air is stagnant, kitchen air is live, thus YIN and YANG clash.)

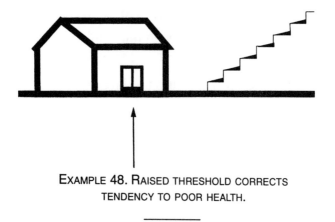

EXAMPLE 48. RAISED THRESHOLD CORRECTS
TENDENCY TO POOR HEALTH.

Indoor arches are for temples and churches. In family homes, they do not promote health and intimacy. On the contrary, arches in a house generate petty arguments within the household, and they undermine the health of the occupants.

Arc shapes belong to the element METAL and for the twenty-year span between 1984 and 2003 METAL lies in the West, and therefore arcs bear no adverse effects. However, from the year 2004 onward, arc doors in family homes will not be desirable features.

The repetitive opening and shutting of elevator doors will adversely affect the fate and fortune of occupants whose door stands exactly opposite. For people

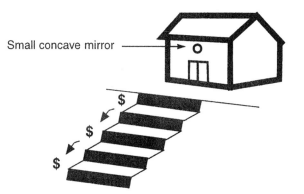

Small concave mirror

EXAMPLE 49. DO NOT LEND MONEY.

who live in apartment houses, this feature can be corrected by placing a convex mirror above the door to deflect the influence of the elevator, and raising the threshold 2 inches above the floor.

When the front door is at the foot of a flight of stairs and stands opposite it (as shown in example 48), occupants will suffer poor health. To correct this, raise the threshold 2-3 inches from the floor.

When the front door is at the top of a flight of stairs (not connected to the house) and directly ahead, money rolls straight out of the front door and down the stairs (see example 49). The occupant will find difficulty hanging on to the fruits of his or her labor. Do not lend money, even to a friend, or you will lose both your money and your friend. To correct this situation, place a concave mirror above the door on the outside of the house. This pulls in the money and keeps it inside the home.

THE INTERACTION OF THE ELEMENTS

In Feng Shui, all things, including people, are classified into one of five elements: WOOD, FIRE, EARTH, METAL, WATER.

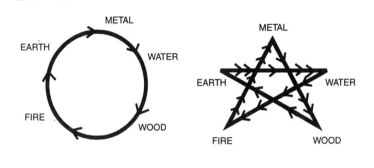

FIGURE 13. COMPATIBILITY (LEFT) AND INCOMPATIBILITY (RIGHT).

These elements represent energies that interact with each other either positively or negatively (see figure 13), or they may simply be neutral to each other, depending on the combination of the energies.

An understanding of how the five elements interact will enable you to pinpoint Feng Shui problems so you can resolve them. For instance, if your element is WATER, wearing an excess of WOOD colors (e.g., green) will drain your energy because wood (trees) soaks up water. On the other hand, the element METAL would support your water element so you'll know to wear white or gold to an interview for example (see figures 14 and 15 on pages 72–73).

Bearing in mind that Feng Shui has to do with the interaction of the Earth, Sun, sky, Moon, stars, and people, we need to harmonize the basic colors of the

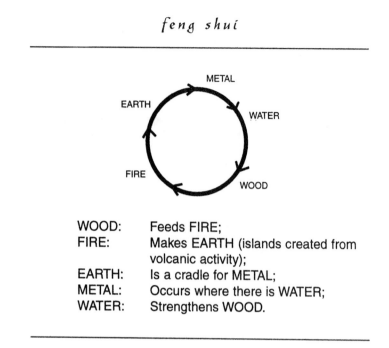

WOOD: Feeds FIRE;
FIRE: Makes EARTH (islands created from volcanic activity);
EARTH: Is a cradle for METAL;
METAL: Occurs where there is WATER;
WATER: Strengthens WOOD.

FIGURE 14. THE INTERACTION OF THE ELEMENTS COMPATIBILITY CYCLE.

elements (namely METAL, WOOD, EARTH, FIRE, WATER) with the interior decor of our dwelling place. The balance can be obtained through the strategic use of shapes, light, and sound.

The shape and color of the door of the house must accord sympathetically with the basic elements of the occupants. To illustrate the point, the son in a particular family had been falling down at school and was always ill. The jinx was the front door which faced North, for North belongs to the element WATER. However, the color of both the door and doormat was

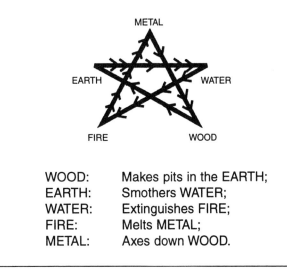

WOOD: Makes pits in the EARTH;
EARTH: Smothers WATER;
WATER: Extinguishes FIRE;
FIRE: Melts METAL;
METAL: Axes down WOOD.

FIGURE 15. INCOMPATIBILITY CYCLE.

green, the color of the element WOOD. The north position was also the direction for the boy, and because WOOD clashed with WATER, the boy had problems.

To correct this problem, have the door painted white (the color of the element METAL), and replace the green doormat with blue (color of the element WATER). These colors of METAL and WATER should support his water element and solve his problems.

In Feng Shui there are eight positions, and these accord with the five elements, as shown in the following examples.

To determine the direction that your front door faces, stand at the doorway, facing the street. If the direction reads West or Northwest, then you have a METAL door, and you can choose the appropriate patterns and color schemes most supportive of this. If the direction reads East, you have a WOOD door. East is also the TONG WAN direction for water; if there is an unpolluted stream in that direction, outside your east-facing door, you can sit back and watch your profits rise. (See also page 76.)

DOORS FACING	BELONG TO	COLORS
East or Southeast	WOOD	Light emerald green
South	FIRE	Red, purple, orange
Southwest or Northeast	EARTH	Yellow or brown
West or Northwest	METAL	White or gold
North	WATER	Black or blue

For front doors facing North, the best colors are those of METAL and WATER (white, gold, and black/blue). Avoid colors of EARTH and WOOD (yellow/brown, and light emerald green). The red/purple/orange of FIRE form neutral colors.

For front doors facing South, the best colors are those of WOOD or FIRE (light emerald green or red/purple/orange). Avoid the colors of WATER and EARTH (blue/black and yellow/brown). The white color of METAL is neutral, and has no adverse effect.

For front doors facing Southwest or Northeast, the best colors are those of FIRE and EARTH (red/purple/orange, and yellow/brown). Avoid colors of WOOD and METAL (light emerald green, gold, and white). The blacks and blues of WATER are neutral.

For front doors facing West or Northwest, the best colors are EARTH and METAL (yellow/brown, and white). Avoid colors of FIRE and WATER (red/purple/orange, and black/blue). Light emerald greens of WOOD are neutral.

For front doors facing East or Southeast, choose colors of WOOD or WATER (light emerald green, or blue/grayish black). Avoid colors of METAL and FIRE (gold/white, and red/purple/orange). EARTH colors of yellow and brown are neutral.

feng shui

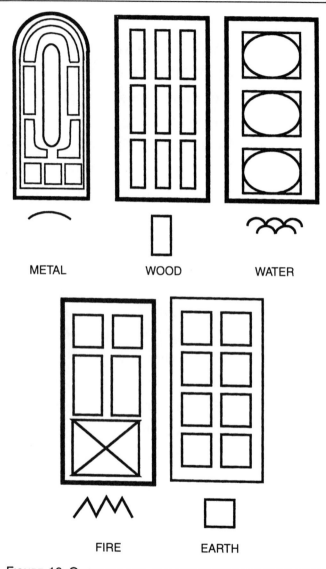

FIGURE 16. ONCE YOU GET ACQUAINTED WITH THE INTERACTION OF THE FIVE ELEMENTS, YOU ARE BETTER ABLE TO CHOOSE DOOR PATTERNS THAT ARE SUPPORTIVE.

• • •

In another instance, a woman noticed that things in her house kept breaking down, such as the washing machine and other electrical appliances. Of late, she herself seemed to have become prone to falls. The problem was caused by the fact that the eaves of the roof across the road were pointing directly at her front door. The position of the front door was in the Southeast, which was also the personal direction of the lady occupant, which accounted for the things happening to her in the house. To correct the situation, hang one set of KEILOON (see page 104 and color insert) on the inside of the front door and place a round convex mirror above the front door to deflect the influence. The effect is to push the influence into the distance, thereby minimizing it. Note that it is okay to have a roof from another house at an angle to your front door; it is only when the eaves point directly at your front door that they become an influence.

CHAPTER 6

Rearranging Interior Decor

To THINK that Feng Shui will give riches beyond dreams is, regrettably, a fallacy. What's yours to have, Feng Shui will help you find, even before you start graying at the temples. However, that which you are not destined to have in the first place, Feng Shui cannot procure for you.

Certainly, Feng Shui can change your luck. For instance, you may be born with a bad lifeline in the palm of your hand, but by attaining an appropriate equilibrium between your living environment and your inner self, you will think positively and generate very positive vibrations. If you communicate this to all you reach, and providing you capitalize on this, you're well and truly launched! Conversely, even if you had a good lifeline but did nothing except lounge around waiting to be showered with unimaginable riches, you could dream your life away!

If you wish to improve and increase your financial situation, always keep the bathroom doors shut. Screen the entrance to your home from the dining room and rooms beyond lest your money escape through the main door. Leave the floor by the entrance uncluttered.

To determine the Dragon or Tiger placement of furniture in the home, which we discuss later in this chapter, you should stand in the center of the room. Face the door of the room you are standing in. To your right is the Tiger and to your left is the Dragon. (See discussion of Tiger and Dragon on pages 47–50.)

Place things constantly in use (clock, radiator, electrical equipment including Nintendo and Sega-Megadrives, etc.) more to the left half of the room, because the left belongs to the Dragon, and is symbolic of power. The wall opposite the door belongs to the Tiger, and must be kept quiet, calm, and static.

FENG SHUI AND LOVE

So how can one tell if a partner is having a "fling on the side" when he or she is meant to be working late? Apart from the obvious weight increase (from having to eat dinner twice), the telltale sign is nothing more

Table 4. The Direction of Birth-Placing Vase.

YEAR	DIRECTION	YEAR	DIRECTION	YEAR	DIRECTION
1941	South	1961	South	1981	South
1942	East	1962	East	1982	East
1943	North	1963	North	1983	North
1944	West	1964	West	1984	West
1945	South	1965	South	1985	South
1946	East	1966	East	1986	East
1947	North	1967	North	1987	North
1948	West	1968	West	1988	West
1949	South	1969	South	1989	South
1950	East	1970	East	1990	East
1951	North	1971	North	1991	North
1952	West	1972	West	1992	West
1953	South	1973	South	1993	South
1954	East	1974	East	1994	East
1955	North	1975	North	1995	North
1956	West	1976	West	1996	West
1957	South	1977	South	1997	South
1958	East	1978	East	1998	East
1959	North	1979	North	1999	North
1960	West	1980	West	2000	West

than an innocent vase placed in a section of a room in the house, which means that your partner may be actively looking for someone new.

To increase your chances of meeting "someone special," or even "any someone," refer to Table 4 (page 81) for your year of birth and the direction that indicates the section of the house where you should place your vase. Fill the vase with water and do not forget to change it every few days.

And if that someone should move in to live with you (or you with him or her) the vase can be safely moved to a new spot.

FENG SHUI AND MARRIAGE

For marital bliss, if you can bury your differences, or even call a truce at the end of the day, you are practically there.

1. Look up your personal Feng Shui direction (chapter 7, pages 108–115).

2. Shift your bed into section 1, 2, 3, or 4 in the relevant Personal Direction Chart (chapter 7, pages 118-121).

THE BEDROOM

The bedroom is understandably associated with rest, relaxation, comfort, and the license to behave freely, since we spend 7-8 hours in bed every day. It follows, therefore, that beds, lights, bureaus, and dressing tables all contribute to a harmonious atmosphere.

HEADBOARDS

Refer to your relevant Personal Direction Chart (pages 118–121). Suppose the inner circle reads "WOOD." If it does, then the type of headboard for you is a square or rectangle. Note that the type of headboard is not an important issue, it is simply an interesting or amusing conversation piece. What is really important is that you position your bed into the relevant section of the bedroom (also shown in the Personal Direction Chart).

In Feng Shui, a round headboard belongs to the element METAL. This is a good shape to make a bee-line for, particularly if you work in an office, and if your personal basic element is METAL, for then you have Feng Shui in doubled strength.

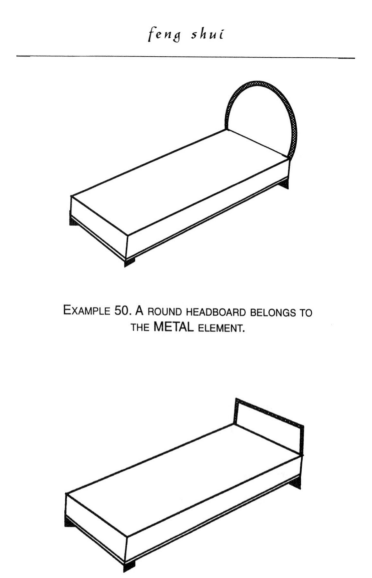

EXAMPLE 50. A ROUND HEADBOARD BELONGS TO THE **METAL** ELEMENT.

EXAMPLE 51. WOOD, EARTH: PROFESSIONALS.

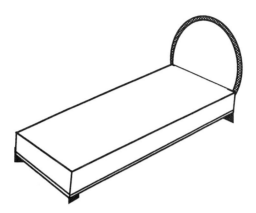

EXAMPLE 52. METAL: OFFICE PEOPLE.

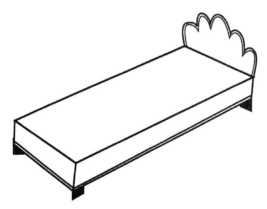

EXAMPLE 53. WATER: MUSICIANS.

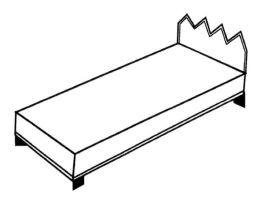

EXAMPLE 54. FIRE: THOSE WHO DO NOT NEED TO SLEEP!

Square or rectangular headboards (example 51) belong to the elements WOOD and EARTH; they are good for professional people.

Round or arc type headboards (example 52) belong to the element METAL. The are not for builders; they are best for office people, or those dealing with paperwork.

Oval or wavy headboards (example 53) belong to the element WATER. They are reserved for artists, musicians, designers.

Sharp pointy zig-zag headboards (example 54) belong to the element FIRE. They are not recommended for anyone.

BEDROOM FURNITURE

Double or bunk beds: Keep in mind that the head of the person on the top bunk must not touch the ceiling when he or she is in a sitting position or he or she will suffer poor health. The tops of mattresses are best 12-14 inches from the ground.

Clocks that are placed immediately behind, or directly in front of, the sleeper are bad Feng Shui. Place them on either side of the bed, but not by the middle section of the bed. Clocks should not be placed in front of writing desks. The person sitting at the desk should not have the clock directly in front of him or her.

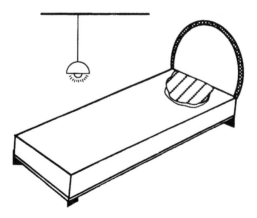

EXAMPLE 55. NO BULB OVER BED.

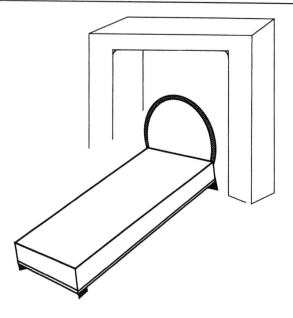

EXAMPLE 56. A FIREPLACE MANTLE IN THE ROOM.

Light bulbs or light fixtures hung above the head of the bed will turn the sleeper into a nervous wreck. If they are hung above the middle section, they will cause stomach disorders. To correct this problem, hang the light elsewhere; to the side of the bed is fine, but not above the bed.

Chimney-breasts or mantles: Many old houses had fireplaces in the bedroom and the mantels are still there. When beds are pushed into chimney-breasts, or even if there is just a mantlepiece above the headboard, success will elude the sleeper.

To correct this situation, place six gold coins on each side of the mantlepiece.

Dressing tables or any other piece of furniture containing a mirror that faces you, when positioned at the foot of the bed, will greatly affect health. Place in any other position.

Doors: if the main entrace to the apartment or house stands directly opposite the bedroom door, this makes the occupant of that bedroom prone to law

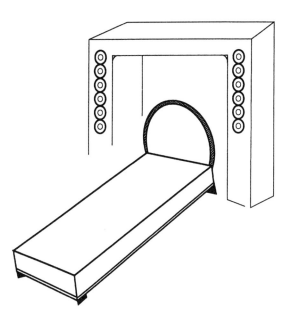

EXAMPLE 57. TO CORRECT FOR A FIREPLACE MANTLE.

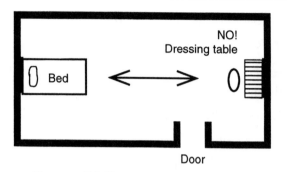

EXAMPLE 58. BAD PLACEMENT OF DRESSER.
KEEP THE MIRROR AWAY FROM YOUR BED!

suits. To correct the situation, place a small ornament, or a piece of furniture, to interrupt the line of passage (flow of Ch'i) from the entrance to the bedroom.

Desks are associated with career. Cabinets and shelves above desks, if built-in as part of the whole

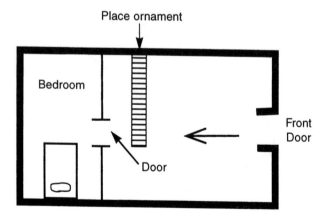

EXAMPLE 59. ENTRANCE TO HOUSE SHOULD NOT BE
OPPOSITE BEDROOM DOOR.

unit, are acceptable, but otherwise shelves above the desk create pressure upon the person at the desk.

The position of the "4 green stars" rules mental activities. This position moves annually. Thus the places for studying for exams are as follows:

1993:	Southwest
1994:	East
1995:	Southeast
1996:	Center
1997:	NORTHWEST
1998:	West
1999:	Northeast
2000:	South
2001:	North

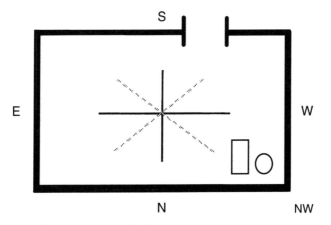

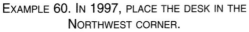

EXAMPLE 60. IN 1997, PLACE THE DESK IN THE NORTHWEST CORNER.

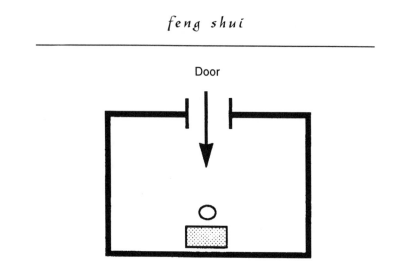

EXAMPLE 61. NOT A GOOD PLACE FOR A DESK.

Desk position is important. A desk placed directly opposite the door (facing it) will affect breathing and concentration.

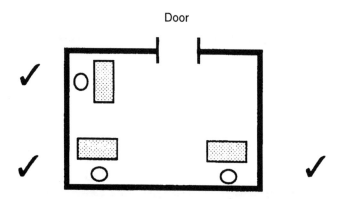

EXAMPLE 62. GOOD DESK PLACEMENT.

Door

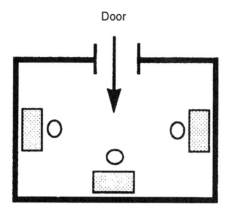

EXAMPLE 63. BAD PLACEMENTS FOR DESKS.

Sitting too close to a door with one's back to the door will affect exam performance.

Sit with your back to the wall. Corners are good positions for desks.

Supporting beams directly above your head, or above the desk, will create pressure and tiredness. A lamp directly above the head numbs concentration. The sitting position should not obstruct doorways. Do not sit too close to the window.

HALLWAY

A shoecase by the entrance along the same wall as the entrance door is fine as long as it is not too high. In

Feng Shui, the space from floor to ceiling is split into three imaginary levels:

Earth,
Human,
and Sky.
} Equidistant

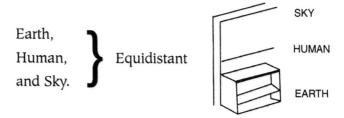

Shoes collect EARTH, so if the shoecase comes up to human level, this will affect the health of the household.

THE LIVING ROOM

Because the living room is the place where occupants gather, the atmosphere is thick with YANG. Clocks, televisions, air-conditioning, and radiators exert a pervasive effect as they are constantly in use. The living room belongs to the element METAL. Having a round clock in gold or white (not silver or chrome) hung in the West or Northwest section of the living room will impart very good luck to the family.

The best position generally for clocks is to the left side of the room and along the same wall as the door into the room.

PAINTINGS FOR THE LIVING ROOM

Fish in movement denotes longevity. Three lambs bears same pronunciation as YANG in YIN/YANG, and are symbolic of light, brightness, and hence, luck. Landscapes depicting morning sunrise, mountains, water, peonies are good. Portraits with a relaxed and smiling countenance are also good.

HOME DECOR

Large paintings having dark, vivid colors in excess, or those of vicious wild beasts, indicate poor health.

Geometrics using very few colors arouse destructive instincts.

Sunsets induce lethargy and end-of-life feelings, or feelings that life is on its last leg. Cascading water is good luck, however.

Excessive red colors are overpowering, and make one irritable. They are fine for temples.

Very big portraits of deceased members of the family evoke too much nostalgia. You want to celebrate life, and encourage positive, forward-looking strides ahead.

PLANTS FOR THE LIVING ROOM

Sharp, spiky leaves—poor health.

Greens, flowers—good. Always remove dead flowers.

Plastic plants—neutral. Does not affect Feng Shui.

Wind chimes on the entrance door invite evil if that door is in the Northeast or Southwest.

SOUVENIRS

Souvenirs from travels, like weapons and carpets, need to be positioned strategically if they are not to attract adverse events.

The Northwest section of the living room belongs to METAL, as do weapons. Excessive METAL leads to a tendency for members of the family to suffer minor injuries to limbs. Place them in a neutral area: East or Southeast.

For red carpets and pictures over four feet in size, with red as the dominant color, avoid the Northwest area, for it belongs to METAL. Red is the color of FIRE; FIRE melts METAL. The East and Southeast belong to

WOOD. FIRE burns WOOD, thus these are undesirable positions for red carpets and red pictures.

Neutral positions are South (which also belongs to FIRE) and North (which belongs to WATER, and therefore holds FIRE in check).

THE DINING ROOM

The use of a dining table as a partition between two rooms is not recommended. A dining table that faces the bathroom door receives too much YIN and affects health.

Dining tables should not be placed directly in front of the main entrance.

If the dining table faces the kitchen, or is located in the kitchen area, it will absorb too much YANG and will give diners a bad temperament. Air conditioning units, central heating, and fans are best placed on the left side of the dining room.

THE KITCHEN

The kitchen is associated with health. The kitchen is the place for the preparation of nourishment, and it will have an effect on your general well-being. The location of kitchen appliances can reduce, obstruct, or induce the free flow of energies. A window opposite the kitchen door is good. Electrical appliances in contant use are best located on the left side of the room.

The worst position for a kitchen in the twenty-year cycle that runs from 1984-2003 is that facing Southwest. If, by coincidence, the stove is situated in the Southwest section of a Southwest-facing kitchen, the occupants will readily fall ill due to digestive disorders. To correct this problem, simply move the stove to any other part of the kitchen. If this is not possible because the stove is inset into a counter, place a small

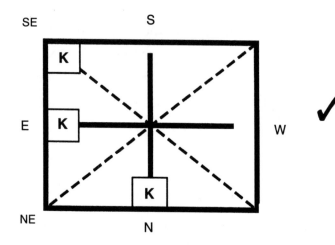

FIGURE 17. GOOD LOCATIONS FOR THE KITCHEN IN A HOUSE.

mirror in such a way that it catches the reflection of the stove and reflects it into another corner of the kitchen.

The kitchen belongs to the element FIRE. The North section of the house belongs to WATER. The East and Southeast sections belong to WOOD. Since fire requires water for cooking, and wood keeps fire burning, assign your kitchens to the North, East, or Southeast section of the house.

The Northeast belongs to the element EARTH, which is neutral.

The Southwest section, as previously mentioned, is not a good position for kitchens.

STOVE

A sink tap pointing to a stove gives rise to stomach upsets. Waterpipes can run under the stove, but not under the floor just below the stove. Shelves above the stove must be at least three feet clear of it.

REFRIGERATOR

Turn the refrigerator doors and the stove doors away from the kitchen door. The refrigerator door should not

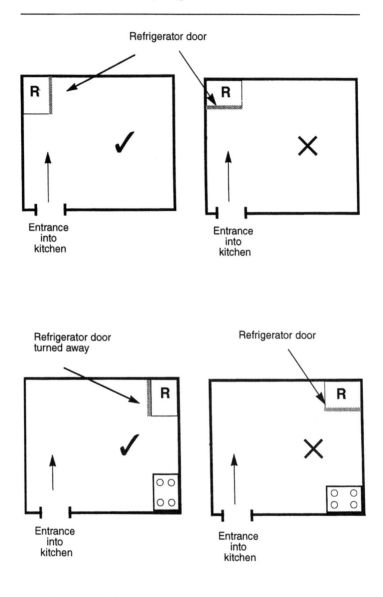

FIGURE 18. POSSIBILITIES FOR CHANGING THE PLACEMENT OF THE REFRIGERATOR IN YOUR KITCHEN.

open facing the kitchen door for the refrigerator is YIN and clashes with people walking in, because people are YANG. Furthermore, the refrigerator doors should not stand directly opposite the stove as "cold" from the refrigerator and "fire" from the stove do not mix. See figure 18.

SINK

Between 1984–2003, the direction for water is East. Therefore the best position for the sink is East. The Southwest is next best. WATER symbolizes money.

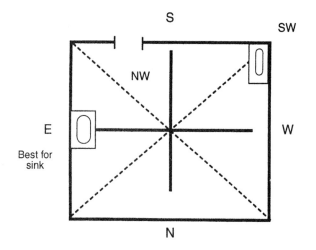

FIGURE 19. KITCHEN PLAN, WITH SINK POSITIONS.

Therefore, a sink to the West means money goes down the drain. Always fix leaking taps promptly.

If you are unable to reposition a badly placed sink, generally ensure that the area around the sink is dry when not in use. Avoid leaving dishes to soak in the sink. If you have to leave glasses or mugs to wash later, first empty the liquid out of them.

SMALL DECORATIVE ITEMS

Putting a horse figure in the south section drastically affects the health of those born in the Year of the Mouse because South (fire) and Mouse (water) clash.

Tiger pictures and decor are totally incompatible with those born in the Year of the Horse and Dog. The tiger pictures affect the health and fortune of those born in the Year of the Horse and Dog, making them prone to litigation and accidents. In Feng Shui we say, "One mountain cannot house two Tigers." So Tiger items are not good for those born in the Year of the Tiger, otherwise they keep running into petty people and obstructions on the workfront.

Monkey also clashes with Tiger, so pictures, paintings, and statuettes of Tigers adversely affect both health and luck of those born in the Year of the Monkey.

Tortoises, on the other hand, signify longevity. Elephants, whether of china, jade, or metal, are good items to place along the wall opposite the door of the living room. The Lion is much prized as the Usherer of Money and should be positioned so that the head of the Lion is turned toward the door.

FISH TANKS AND AQUARIUMS

These are conducive to healthy finances, as moving water circulates the flow of money. The left side of the room is a good position.

DRAGONS

You will always see embroidered Dragons on the clothes belonging to an emperor. The Dragon is power. Do not place a dragon on the right-hand side of a room for its power is neutralized in this position.

KEILOON

The Keiloon is a legendary creature with horns on the head of a lion, scales upon the body of a deer, and a tail consisting of little curls. Legend has it that this creature eats wicked people. Tricksters, thieves, and murderers should not hang this by their doors as they, themselves, will get "eaten."

Placed at the front door, mouth facing the door, the Keiloon is the sentinel that neutralizes any harm-

KEILOON. THE THREE ANCIENT COINS YOU SEE SLUNG ACROSS ITS BACK REPRESENT CHARMS FROM PAST EMPERORS. KEILOONS ARE USUALLY MADE FROM BRASS OR COPPER.

ful element entering the home. It has a health-giving effect upon the house.

If the Feng Shui positioning of a house is unfavorable, the Keiloon will dilute any adverse energies circulating around the house.

THE OTHER MEMBERS OF THE FAMILY

Our feline friends belong to the element WOOD. Thus the colors for their blankets are blue, black, or green. Do not use red. Front doors opening to North, East, South, and Northwest make cats very strong and healthy. Front doors that face the Northeast and Southwest do not make good openings for cats.

Our canine companions belong to the element EARTH. METAL detracts from EARTH, so white baskets make dogs ill. Front doors opening into the Northwest, East, and South make the dog strong, while those facing Southeast and Northeast make it feel poorly.

CHAPTER 7

Birth Year Personal Direction Table

T HERE MAY be instances where a house is a really good house for you but is not necessarily so compatible for the other occupants. By using the Birth Year Direction Table (see Table 5 on pages 108–115) and the Personal Direction Chart (see pages 118–121), you can ascertain which rooms are most appropriate for each individual and can therefore be allocated to them as their bedrooms. Next, proceed to Feng Shui the rest of the house in favor of the main breadwinner.

In the Personal Direction Charts, the symbols ⊢ and ⟶ for each directional chart show the ideal position when you are choosing your site. This chart includes your direction and your element, as well as numbers and letters that you can interpret.

Table 5. Birth Year Directions.

YEAR OF BIRTH	MALE	FEMALE
1901	South	Northwest
1902	Northeast	West
1903	West	Northeast
1904	Northwest	South
1905	Southwest	North
1906	Southeast	Southwest
1907	East	East
1908	Southwest	Southeast
1909	North	Northeast
1910	South	Northwest
1911	Northeast	West
1912	West	Northeast
1913	Northwest	South
1914	Southwest	North
1915	Southeast	Southwest

Table 5. Birth Year Directions (cont.).

YEAR OF BIRTH	MALE	FEMALE
1916	East	East
1917	Southwest	Southeast
1918	North	Northeast
1919	South	Northwest
1920	Northeast	West
1921	West	Northeast
1922	Northwest	South
1923	Southwest	North
1924	Southeast	Southwest
1925	East	East
1926	Southwest	Southeast
1927	North	Northeast
1928	South	Northwest
1929	Northeast	West
1930	West	Northeast

feng shui

Table 5. Birth Year Directions (cont.).

YEAR OF BIRTH	MALE	FEMALE
1931	Northwest	South
1932	Southwest	North
1933	Southeast	Southwest
1934	East	East
1935	Southwest	Southeast
1936	North	Northeast
1937	South	Northwest
1938	Northeast	West
1939	West	Northeast
1940	Northwest	South
1941	Southwest	North
1942	Southeast	Southwest
1943	East	East
1944	Southwest	Southeast
1945	North	Northeast

Table 5. Birth Year Directions (cont.).

YEAR OF BIRTH	MALE	FEMALE
1946	South	Northwest
1947	Northeast	West
1948	West	Northeast
1949	Northwest	South
1950	Southwest	North
1951	Southeast	Southwest
1952	East	East
1953	Southwest	Southeast
1954	North	Northeast
1955	South	Northwest
1956	Northeast	West
1957	West	Northeast
1958	Northwest	South
1959	Southwest	North
1960	Southeast	Southwest

Table 5. Birth Year Directions (cont.).

YEAR OF BIRTH	MALE	FEMALE
1961	East	East
1962	Southwest	Southeast
1963	North	Northeast
1964	South	Northwest
1965	Northeast	West
1966	West	Northeast
1967	Northwest	South
1968	Southwest	North
1969	Southeast	Southwest
1970	East	East
1971	Southwest	Southeast
1972	North	Northeast
1973	South	Northwest
1974	Northeast	West
1975	West	Northeast

Table 5. Birth Year Directions (cont.).

YEAR OF BIRTH	MALE	FEMALE
1976	Northwest	South
1977	Southwest	North
1978	Southeast	Southwest
1979	East	East
1980	Southwest	Southeast
1981	North	Northeast
1982	South	Northwest
1983	Northeast	West
1984	West	Northeast
1985	Northwest	South
1986	Southwest	North
1987	Southeast	Southwest
1988	East	East
1989	Southwest	Southeast
1990	North	Northeast

Table 5. Birth Year Directions (cont.).

YEAR OF BIRTH	MALE	FEMALE
1991	South	Northwest
1992	Northeast	West
1993	West	Northeast
1994	Northwest	South
1995	Southwest	North
1996	Northeast	Southwest
1997	East	East
1998	Southwest	Southeast
1999	North	Northeast
2000	South	Northwest
2001	Southeast	West
2002	West	Northeast
2003	Northwest	South
2004	Southwest	North
2005	Southeast	Southwest

Table 5. Birth Year Directions (cont.).

YEAR OF BIRTH	MALE	FEMALE
2006	East	East
2007	Southwest	Southeast
2008	North	Northeast
2009	South	Northwest
2010	Northeast	West
2011	West	Northeast
2012	Northwest	South
2013	Southwest	North
2014	Southeast	Southwest
2015	East	East
2016	Southwest	Southeast
2017	North	Northeast
2018	South	Northwest
2019	Northeast	West
2020	West	Northeast

If your house does not correspond to the suggested ideals, all is not lost. Further, it is also unlikely to be aligned in the most auspicious direction for the present twenty-year cycle, with doors correctly oriented for both Air and Water. How then, will you "change your life"?

The answer lies in the positioning of your bed and your desk. Move these out of sections marked A, B, C, D in your Personal Direction Chart and into section 1. If that is not possible, then try for sections 2, 3, or 4. Your bed is your energizer, from where you wake up feeling lethargic, or revitalized and "ready to go." That particular day may well be The Day For Big Decisions, when the principle of being in the right place at the right time really counts.

HOW TO READ THE PERSONAL DIRECTION CHART

In the Personal Direction Chart, the numbers 1-4 represent four beneficial winds. The letters A-D represent four adverse influences. The beneficial winds offer the following benefits:

1—Prosperous Wind: excellent financial position, health, vital energy;

2—Yearly Progress: denotes wealth, longevity, good health;

3—Good Doctor: imparts speedy recovery from illnesses, people around are helpful, financial position is stable;

4—Good Seat: enjoys ordinary wealth, luck, and health.

The corresponding four adverse influences, represented alphabetically as A, B, C, D, give:

A—Bad Life: poverty, illness, sometimes even death;

B—Ghosts: financial losses, poor health, easily jinxed;

C—Bad Influences: always jinxed, health and financial positions not good;

D—Disaster: unable to retain money, frequently engaged in arguments, litigation, and being shouted at.

When reading Personal Direction Charts, stand in the center of your bedroom and mark down the sections of the room corresponding to the compass (the good and bad areas according to the chart).

PERSONAL DIRECTION CHARTS

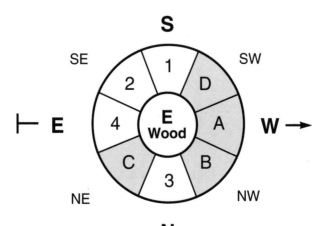

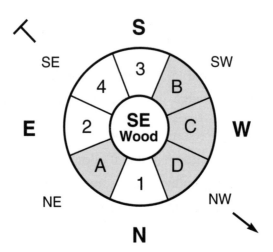

PERSONAL DIRECTION CHARTS

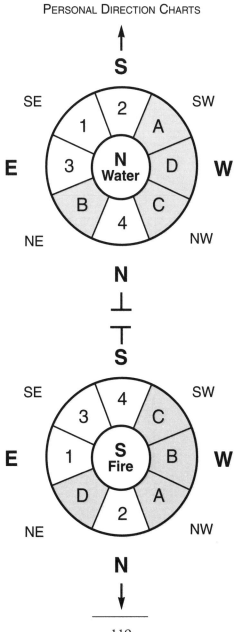

PERSONAL DIRECTION CHARTS

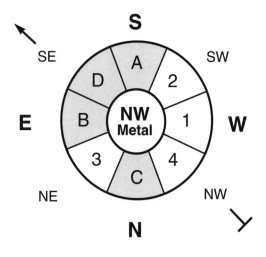

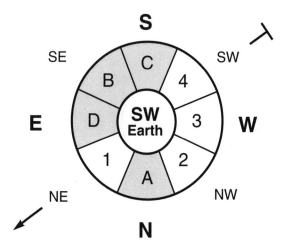

PERSONAL DIRECTION CHARTS

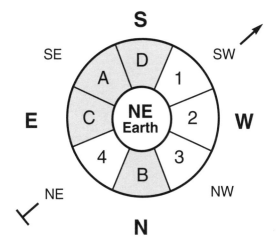

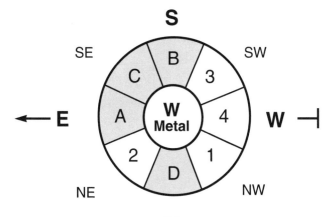

CHAPTER 8

Calculations

WE HAVE included some examples to help readers learn how to find the best Feng Shui for themselves. For example, pretend you are a woman born in 1958.

1. Find your personal Feng Shui direction according to your year of birth (Table 5, pages 108–115). For 1958 your direction is South.

2. Next find the Personal Direction Chart (see pages 118–121) that shows your personal direction "S" (South) in the inner circle. The Personal Direction Chart for a woman born in 1958 shows the personal Feng Shui direction is South, belonging to the element FIRE. The directions marked 1-4 indicate beneficial winds; A, B, C, D indicate the direction of adversity.

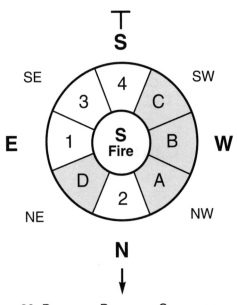

FIGURE 20. PERSONAL DIRECTION CHART FOR A WOMAN BORN IN 1958.

For an explanation of the direction in the Personal Direction Chart, see pages 116-117.

3. If a woman born in 1958 is looking for a house, her Personal Direction Chart indicates the ideal direction for the house has the entrance door facing North ⟶. The back of the house faces South ⊢.

If the house has already been purchased and is not placed in the ideal direction (as is often the case), then use the openings shown in sections 1, 2, 3, or 4 in the relevant Personal Direction Chart as the main entrance.

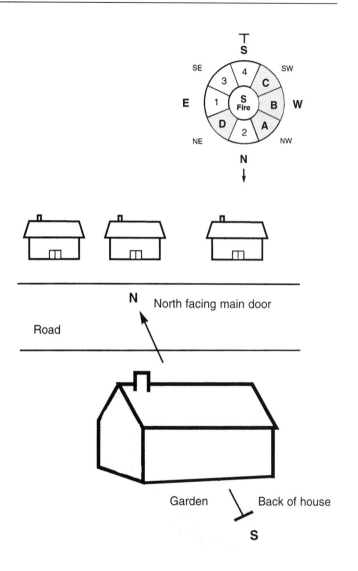

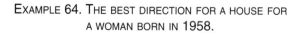

EXAMPLE 64. THE BEST DIRECTION FOR A HOUSE FOR A WOMAN BORN IN 1958.

The birth year and Personal Direction Chart works differently for a man born in 1958. Look up the birth year on page 111.

1. The Feng Shui Direction Table for a man born in 1958 will read Northwest.

2. Find the Personal Direction Chart that shows his personal direction "NW" in the inner circle (see page 120). The Personal Direction Chart belongs to the element METAL. Directions marked 1-4 indicate beneficial winds; A, B, C, D indicate adversity (see pages 116–117).

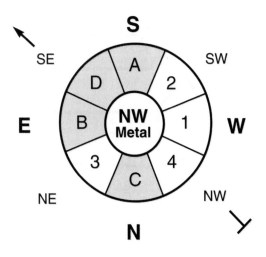

FIGURE 21. PERSONAL DIRECTION CHART FOR A MAN BORN IN 1958.

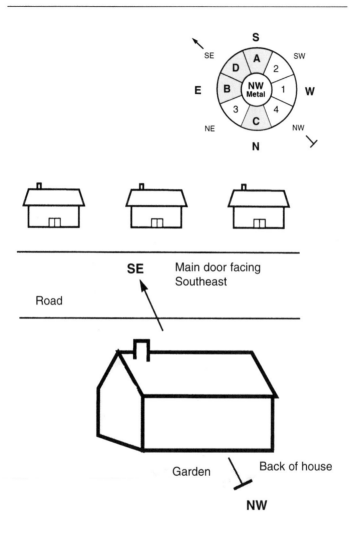

EXAMPLE 65. THE BEST DIRECTION FOR A HOUSE FOR
A MAN BORN IN 1958.

3. According to the Personal Direction Chart for a man born in 1958, the ideal direction for his house has the main door facing Southeast ⟶ and the back of the house facing Northwest ⊢.

Note that the Southeast quadrant is "D" (not desirable). This is fine because the back of the house to the Northwest and facing Southeast is the ideal direction for a house when the man is born in 1958. For his well-being (or good life direction), he should choose a room with the door facing 1, 2, 3, or 4 for his bedroom, as shown in the Personal Direction Chart.

4. To ascertain which room directions are most appropriate for particular individuals, place that individual's Personal Direction Chart on a spot in the center of the house. The directions marked 1-4 may be allocated as his or her bedroom.

5. Now proceed to Feng Shui the rest of the house in favor of the Head of the House. Place his or her Personal Direction Chart in the center of all the other rooms in the house and Feng Shui from there.

HOW DIRECTIONS AFFECT
MEMBERS OF THE FAMILY

Now and then a member of the family may be going through a short spell of bad luck, poor health, or the like. To help concentrate his or her energies, find the areas within the house specific to the individual, and balance the Feng Shui. For example, if the eldest son deals in the stock exchange, move red-colored carpets away from the East section of the rooms that he spends most of his time in. The following directions will help you determine the areas in the house that will help balance the individual.

East: Reserved for the eldest son, and men in the household aged 31-45 years.

Southeast: For the eldest daughter, and women in the household aged 31-45 years.

South: For women aged 16-30 years.

Southwest: Belongs to the mother and women aged 46+ years.

West: Belongs to girls aged 1-15 years.

Northwest:	Belongs to the father and men aged 46+ years.
North:	Belongs to men aged 16-30 years.
Northeast:	Belongs to boys aged 1-15 years.

Specific areas in the home relate to different individuals. The use of color may support or detract from the energies of the individual associated with a certain area. Items of decoration (listed below) may include small items or even wallpaper, carpets, rugs, floormats. An overall predominance of the appropriate color is all that you need. See Table 6 on pages 131–133.

Remember that all things, including people, belong to one of the five elements: METAL, WOOD, WATER, FIRE, EARTH. The use of color scheme in interior decoration is an effective tool in Feng Shui.

Feng Shui encompasses a combination of diverse aspects which are woven together into the whole scheme. Thus, when using colors one must understand the distinction between colors associated with people (i.e., their personal elements), colors favoring a certain direction (see page 74: WATER colors, such as

Table 6. Color Feng Shui.

Direction in Home	Corresponding Individuals
East	Eldest son and men aged 31-45 years. Use WATER colors. Blue and black items of decoration placed in these areas in the home will enhance the energies of these individuals. Keep red colors in these sections to a minimum.
Southeast	Eldest daughter and women aged 31-45 years. WATER colors, and blue and black decorations will help. Keep red to a minimum.
South	Women aged 16-30 years. FIRE colors (red, orange, purple) are best. Avoid WATER decorations (blacks and blues).

Table 6. Color Feng Shui (cont.).

DIRECTION IN HOME	CORRESPONDING INDIVIDUALS
Southwest	Mother and women aged 46+ years. EARTH colors—browns and yellows are best. Avoid predominantly white, gold, or METAL colors.
Northeast	Boys aged 1-15 years. Introduce EARTH colors (yellows and browns). Predominantly white or gold colors are undesirable.
West	Girls aged 1-15 years. Good colors are metallic golds and white. Avoid red, orange, and purple.
Northwest	Father and men aged 46+ years. Beneficial colors are whites and yellows. Avoid a predominence of orange, red, and purple.

Table 6. Color Feng Shui (cont.).

DIRECTION IN HOME	CORRESPONDING INDIVIDUALS
North	Men aged 16-30 years. Supportive colors are METAL white and gold; yellows and greens are not.

black and blue, are for North-facing doors), and colors relating to specific areas in the home independently of the occupants' own personal elements. Table 6 shows that items of decoration in WATER colors, such as black and blue, belong to the East and Southeast sections of the home.

Do not confuse these categories of application. They are separate. Although it may coincidentally happen that one color may satisfy two or more categories, the categories, nevertheless, remain distinct.

To illustrate this point, say you are the eldest son, and your personal element is FIRE. Hence colors of FIRE, such as red, orange, and purple, would be supportive of your element. These are the colors you would wear for an important occasion. WATER colors (blue and black) would only detract from your FIRE element. Nevertheless, in the section of the home relating to the eldest son (i.e., East), the reverse would hold true, and WATER colors would be beneficial. In other words, in the specific areas in the home the individual would use the WATER colors, and not the colors of the individual's own personal element.

CHAPTER 9

General Feng Shui for Your Home

FENG SHUI has to do with calculating directions in relation to the Earth's energy meridian, and is also based on the interplay of the five elements. As the Earth turns upon its axis, so the directions for energy pathways also change with the astral and magnetic influences. Thus, provided that you know which direction your front door faces, it is possible to determine which energy will dominate the house in a given year, or even over a twenty-year cycle.

On the pages that follow, we will describe the next few years. We start with 1996, so that when you first read this book, you can see how the past has affected you. Then you can make plans to change your future, and make sure that Feng Shui is working for you.

Our new year starts on February 10th, so the beginning of 1997 is February 10th, and not January 1st. These influences will affect your home regardless of when you were born, how many people live in the house, or other personal factors. Obviously your own personal factors will develop this "plan" more specifically, but this outline will give you a general idea of the energy available to you.

You will note that we refer to both the front door and the bedroom door in our forecasting. You will be using both energies here. If your front door faces one direction, that is what is in store'for you. If your bedroom door faces another direction, then read that section, as well.

The main door (or front door) refers to the main entrance to your house or apartment. Whether or not it faces the street is irrelevant. The following corrective measures will reduce any adverse influences by as much as 80 percent.

General Feng Shui for Homes for 1996

1996: FRONT DOOR OR BEDROOM DOOR
FACING SOUTH

These doors invite prosperity, particularly for those in business and property. To enhance this good fortune, place a fish tank (six fishes) by the front door (whether to the right or left hand side is irrelevant). Remove any metal decorations or plants from the front door. Instead, introduce a blue or black doormat just inside the door.

Smooth-going and a definite improvement in money matters will accrue for those whose bedroom doors face South. However, between November 7 and December 6, 1996, people with South-facing bedroom doors should place a red doormat (or rug) just inside the bedroom door to ward off minor accidents.

1996: FRONT DOOR OR BEDROOM DOOR
FACING SOUTHEAST

This door configuration spells bickering and conflict. The occupants will find themselves involved in protracted arguments. Also, others will gossip behind their backs. Avoid having any building or gardening work near the front door for 1996, as it could make these household accident-prone.

1996: FRONT DOOR OR BEDROOM DOOR FACING SOUTHWEST

This door arrangement promises good luck and romance for 1996. For those who are unmarried and wish to meet a new partner, place a big vase full of colorful flowers in the Southwest section of your living-room.

If you are trying for a baby boy, move your bed to the Southwest section of the bedroom and place a blue carpet underneath it.

1996: FRONT DOOR OR BEDROOM DOOR FACING NORTH

Happy news awaits occupants at this door. Place a pink or purple carpet at the front door to enhance this lucky star. Now is also the moment to drag your bed to the North section of the room, stand it on a red carpet, and try for a baby girl.

1996: FRONT DOOR OR BEDROOM DOOR FACING NORTHWEST

Roadwork, construction on the building, or digging near the main door will expose you to a high probability of getting burgled. Remove all decorative items and red colors from there as these will adversely affect your health and financial situation.

To dilute this negative energy, and prevent losses in income, paint the main door white and hang a KEILOON on either side of the main door (the mouth of the Keiloon to face the door). Also, place a white or cream-colored rug or doormat immediately inside the main door.

If your bedroom door faces Northwest, move the bed out of the Northwest section of the room. Further, do not place your desk in any room in the Northwest section of the home.

1996: FRONT DOOR OR BEDROOM DOOR FACING WEST

People whose front door or bedroom door faces West will travel more frequently this year. To increase your income, place a brown doormat just inside your front door. For good luck, place a metal horse in the West side of your livingroom. Avoid having fish tanks in your home this year or you may lose your money. This is an auspicious year for those in the travel business.

1996: FRONT DOOR OR BEDROOM DOOR FACING NORTHEAST

A year of plenty, particularly for those in catering or the entertainment business. Avoid having red carpets and decoration at the front door, as these will cast a shadow on your good fortune. To protect from fraudsters, introduce a pair of Keiloons by the door. For an even bigger boost, place a round brass clock in the Northeast section of the living room.

1996: FRONT DOOR OR BEDROOM DOOR FACING EAST

During 1996, this door lies in the path of the "star of ill health." To minimize health problems, place six gold coins (brass is also fine, it is the gold color that matters, not the content) on each side of the East-facing door. If the kitchen is located in the East section of the home, this will aggravate skin problems. Go easy on the stomach with regard to food and drink.

Keep activity in the East section of the home to a minimum. Do not place the television, sofa, or a fish tank on the East side of the home.

This is a good year for lawyers and those working in the health professions.

General Feng Shui for Homes for 1997

1997: FRONT DOOR OR BEDROOM DOOR FACING EAST

These doors are well-positioned to catch the energy for happiness, love, and travel during 1997. If your front door or bedroom door faces East, placing a blue doormat (or area rug) immediately *inside* it will amplify this beneficial energy.

1997: FRONT DOOR OR BEDROOM DOOR FACING SOUTHEAST

During 1997, people (particularly women age 31-45 years) with doors facing Southeast may experience health problems. To correct this imbalance of energies, place six gold-colored coins (gold or brass is fine) on each side of the Southeast-facing door.

If the kitchen is located in the East section of the home, go easy on the stomach with regard to food and drink. Keep activity in the East section of the home to a minimum. Do not place the television, sofa, or a fish tank on the East side of the home. This is a good year for those working in the health professions.

1997: FRONT DOOR OR BEDROOM DOOR
FACING SOUTH

During 1997, this door arrangement makes occupants prone to gossip, lawsuits, and burglary. Avoid having clocks in the South section of your home, and keep activity in that area down to a minimum.

Remedial measures: Do not sit with your back to a window, but rather against a wall or screen. This will check or curb the gossip. Invest in good door locks! Place a brown or yellow doormat just *inside* your South-facing front door or bedroom door.

1997: FRONT DOOR OR BEDROOM DOOR
FACING SOUTHWEST

1997 offers a triple bonus: a bright outlook in luck, financial prospects, and career. This is a hectic, but rewarding, year. To enhance your good fortune, place a green carpet *inside* these doors.

1997: FRONT DOOR OR BEDROOM DOOR
FACING WEST

During 1997, there is more negative energy at these doors. To dilute this negative energy and prevent loses of income, paint the main door white and hang a

KEILOON on either side of the main door (the mouth of the Keiloon to face the door). Place a white or cream-colored rug or doormat immediately *inside* the front door. Remove all decorative items, plants, and red colors from there, as these will adversely affect your financial situation and health.

If possible, avoid having roadwork, building construction, or digging near the front door for this year. Also, move beds and desks out of the Northwest section of the home or from any room that has a West-facing door.

1997: FRONT DOOR OR BEDROOM DOOR FACING NORTHWEST

These doors are well-positioned to catch the "Four Green Stars" that boost education and career. Introduce water plants at the front door. This energy will focus concentration and stimulate creativity. Place a green doormat just *inside* these doors and move desks into the Northwest section of the home.

1997: FRONT DOOR OR BEDROOM DOOR
FACING NORTH

These are the most auspicious doors for 1997, and particularly so for people in the catering business. This beneficial energy brings prosperity, good luck, and career opportunities. A pink, brown, or yellow carpet at the front door will keep this energy active.

1997: FRONT DOOR OR BEDROOM DOOR
FACING NORTHEAST

The "Star for Travel" insures opportunities for travel. This is also a good year if you are moving house or offices. Place a black or navy blue doormat at the front door to combat proneness to a lawsuit.

Those in the travel or courier services, including long-distance drivers, will see an increase in income.

General Feng Shui for Homes for 1998

1998: FRONT DOOR OR BEDROOM DOOR
FACING SOUTH

An auspicious year for those in the travel business. You should take care to move any fish tanks away from the South part of the house during 1998 as these could reduce your financial good fortune. For good luck, place six very old gold-colored coins on each side of the South-facing door.

1998: FRONT DOOR OR BEDROOM DOOR
FACING SOUTHWEST

This year will be smooth going, particular for business and career-minded people. Remove plants or any green-colored objects from the area of the door to minimize any negative energies there may be. A red doormat, or a fish tank with six fish near the front door will enhance all the positive energies around in 1998.

1998: FRONT DOOR OR BEDROOM DOOR
FACING WEST

West-facing doors are well-placed in 1998 to catch the beneficial winds of the "Four Green Stars," which can have a positive effect on financial circumstances, particularly for teachers or those working in offices. To capitalize on this, place a dark green doormat at the front door, or put plants anywhere in the door area.

1998: FRONT DOOR OR BEDROOM DOOR FACING NORTHWEST

1998's configuration for houses with Northwest-facing doors indicates the possibility of conflict and argument. Minimize the negative energies by placing a red or orange-colored doormat inside the front door and remove any green plants.

1998: FRONT DOOR OR BEDROOM DOOR FACING NORTH

This is not the most auspicious direction for the front door in 1998, as there are potentially invasive energies denoting the possibility of poor financial luck. Place a white doormat just inside the door and a KEILOON on each side of the door to enhance the positive energies.

1998: FRONT DOOR OR BEDROOM DOOR
FACING NORTHEAST

Negative energies in these homes may affect both health and finances in 1998. To correct these influences, place six very old gold-colored coins on each side of the door, or place a KEILOON on each side of the door, with the faces toward the door. Painting the door white and placing a white doormat inside the door will also deflect the negative energies.

1998: FRONT DOOR OR BEDROOM DOOR
FACING EAST

In 1998, there will be happy news for those whose front door or bedroom door faces East, and their luck will be good. Place a green rug or doormat just *inside* the door to enhance the good fortune still further.

1998: FRONT DOOR OR BEDROOM DOOR
FACING SOUTHEAST

In 1998, occupants of houses with Southeast-facing doors will catch the energy for happiness, love, and travel. Place a blue doormat inside the door to maximize your chances of success in love and romance.

General Feng Shui for Homes for 1999

1999: FRONT DOOR OR BEDROOM DOOR FACING NORTHWEST

For 1999, the energy at these door is that of illness. Those prone to coughs, colds, and minor aches and pains will suffer from these more this year than in other years. Make a conscious effort to keep to a balanced diet. Not having too many red decorations at the front door will help.

1999: FRONT DOOR OR BEDROOM DOOR FACING WEST

1999 is your turn to be the subject of gossip. To negate this energy, place a red doormat just inside these doors, and remove any plants by the door. Try to keep company with people whose advice is lucky for you.

1999: FRONT DOOR OR BEDROOM DOOR FACING NORTHEAST

Round-leafed, succulent plants by these doors will help you make the most of this energy for career and promotion prospects. If, however, there is a lamppost both directly in line with, and very close by, the front door, place a red doormat at the front door instead of plants. To focus this energy for knowledge and artistic creativity, place your work desk in the Northeast section of your home.

1999: FRONT DOOR OR BEDROOM DOOR FACING SOUTH

There is a negative energy at these doors. It is best to refrain from making big investment decisions this year. Rather, concentrate on your health and make time for relaxation, so that when the energy for a brighter outlook arrives at this door in 2000, you will be re-energized and ready to take full advantage of it. To counter the adverse energy, place a pair of KEILOONS (made of either brass or copper) by the front door.

1999: FRONT DOOR OR BEDROOM DOOR FACING NORTH

The energy here for 1999 is related to "movement," so if you had been intending to move home or office, chances are that you would find yourself doing so this year. 1999 offers opportunities for travel. For those who are vulnerable to head and lung problems, such as migraine, chronic cough, etc., introduce a water plant at your North-facing front door.

1999: FRONT DOOR OR BEDROOM DOOR FACING SOUTHWEST

The good news is that financial prospects are very good. The bad news is that this same energy also makes you prone to burglary. To accentuate this money energy, place a brown or yellow doormat or rug near the front door.

1999: FRONT DOOR OR BEDROOM DOOR FACING EAST

This aspect attracts beneficial energy, and occupants at this door can expect unexpected windfalls. To maximize this potential, move desks and beds into the East section of the home. Also, introduce Earth colors (browns, yellows) near the front door area.

1999: FRONT DOOR OR BEDROOM DOOR
FACING SOUTHEAST

This door configuration offers good news, a marriage, and perhaps even a baby. Give an added boost to this energy by introducing a red or purple doormat just inside the front door. You might also like to place your bed on a red carpet.

General Feng Shui for Homes for 2000

2000: FRONT DOOR OR BEDROOM DOOR FACING NORTHWEST

For those who have been putting off plans to travel, this is the time for wanderlust. It is also a good year for moving offices, and making business trips. However, this energy makes those in the 16-30 year old age group (and also persons in frail health) vulnerable to minor problems related to the blood, kidneys, and ears. To alleviate this, check that your bed is not in the Northwest section of the bedroom and, if your bedroom door faces Northwest, place a green doormat just inside the door.

2000: FRONT DOOR OR BEDROOM DOOR FACING WEST

For this year the energy here gives ill health arising from stomach complaints and eczema. An effective remedial measure is to hang a pair of brass KEILOONS, one on either side of the bedroom door, and stop being such a worrier!

2000: FRONT DOOR OR BEDROOM DOOR FACING NORTHEAST

2000 finds "argument" energy at these doors. People argue with you, or else they gossip behind your back. Introduce a FIRE-colored (i.e., red) doormat just inside these doors to burn down those aggravations. Remove plants from these doors.

2000: FRONT DOOR OR BEDROOM DOOR FACING SOUTH

The year 2000 will find your creative energy at its peak, as the energy that stimulates knowledge and education takes position at these doors. Shift your work desks into the South section of the home, and introduce a landscape picture with blue skies and water and greenery by these doors.

2000: FRONT DOOR OR BEDROOM DOOR FACING NORTH

The energy here for this year is negative. Therefore, save your big decision-making and house-hunting for when the energy level is more favorable. Station your KEILOONS at your front door as a buffer against burglary, retrieve from the attic all those books you meant to read, but never could find the time for, go on a vacation, generally use this year to re-energize.

2000: FRONT DOOR OR BEDROOM DOOR FACING SOUTHWEST

A hectic year ahead, though not particularly fantastic or bad.

2000: FRONT DOOR OR BEDROOM DOOR FACING EAST

The year 2000 will see healthy finances and promotion prospects for occupants passing through these doors. To enhance this beneficial energy, place a round, brass clock in the East section of your living room.

2000: FRONT DOOR OR BEDROOM DOOR FACING SOUTHEAST

Doors turned toward this direction attract both good fortune, health, and wealth. To stimulate this energy, introduce happy colors of red, orange, or purple by these doors.

Chinese Signs and Elements

FENG SHUI concerns itself with people and their interaction with Earth, Sun, sky, Moon, and stars. Everything, including people, is classified into one of the five elements: WOOD, FIRE, EARTH, METAL, WATER. And each of the five elements has particular characteristics. These can each be energizing or debilitating, according to how they interact with each other.

As you come to understand more about the ancient Chinese art of Feng Shui, you will increasingly be able to recognize the symbolic nature of its many aspects. Thinking about the physical qualities of the element gives a good indication of their psychological attributes and energy qualities. The following list describes personality traits. While description has more to do with fortune telling than with Feng Shui, and has nothing to do with personal Feng Shui, it may help you understand certain types of people.

Wood: These people have a strong personality. However, they can be easily influenced. They are helpful toward others, but tend to be fearful that others will try to control them, or order them about.

Fire: These people are generous in friendship, and always try to help, but they tend to be unable to look after themselves.

Earth: These people are kind-hearted and always keep their word. On the other hand, they dislike advice and can be liable to change their minds.

Metal: These people spend money like water. By nature, they are generous, brave, and helpful. Don't expect them to form long term perspectives, or to take kindly to losing face!

Water: These people are never petty. They are clever people and plan well ahead; however, they tend to be faint-hearted.

CHINESE ANIMAL SIGNS

According to your animal sign, your personality will show specific characteristics. These will be further modified by the element relating to the year of your birth. In addition to this, you will exhibit other characteristics—both physically and in your personality—which relate to one particular element. If you visit a Chinese herbalist or acupuncturist, he or she will probably diagnose your "personality" element from these individual factors. Table 7 explains the elements for the year in relationship to the Chinese astrological signs.

Table 7. Chinese Signs and Elements

Year of Birth	Element	Chinese Astrological Sign
1914	Wood	Tiger
1915	Wood	Rabbit
1916	Earth	Dragon
1917	Fire	Snake
1918	Fire	Horse
1919	Earth	Goat
1920	Metal	Monkey
1921	Metal	Rooster
1922	Earth	Dog

Table 7. Chinese Signs and Elements (cont.).

YEAR OF BIRTH	ELEMENT	CHINESE ASTROLOGICAL SIGN
1923	Water	Pig
1924	Water	Rat
1925	Earth	Ox
1926	Wood	Tiger
1927	Wood	Rabbit
1928	Earth	Dragon
1929	Fire	Snake
1930	Fire	Horse
1931	Earth	Goat
1932	Metal	Monkey
1933	Metal	Rooster
1934	Earth	Dog
1935	Water	Pig
1936	Water	Rat
1937	Earth	Ox
1938	Wood	Tiger
1939	Wood	Rabbit
1940	Earth	Dragon

Table 7. Chinese Signs and Elements (cont.).

Year of Birth	Element	Chinese Astrological Sign
1941	Fire	Snake
1942	Fire	Horse
1943	Earth	Goat
1944	Metal	Monkey
1945	Metal	Rooster
1946	Earth	Dog
1947	Water	Pig
1948	Water	Rat
1949	Earth	Ox
1950	Wood	Tiger
1951	Wood	Rabbit
1952	Earth	Dragon
1953	Fire	Snake
1954	Fire	Horse
1955	Earth	Goat
1956	Metal	Monkey
1957	Metal	Rooster
1958	Earth	Dog

Table 7. Chinese Signs and Elements (cont.).

YEAR OF BIRTH	ELEMENT	CHINESE ASTROLOGICAL SIGN
1959	Water	Pig
1960	Water	Rat
1961	Earth	Ox
1962	Wood	Tiger
1963	Wood	Rabbit
1964	Earth	Dragon
1965	Fire	Snake
1966	Fire	Horse
1967	Earth	Goat
1968	Metal	Monkey
1969	Metal	Rooster
1970	Earth	Dog
1971	Water	Pig
1972	Water	Rat
1973	Earth	Ox
1974	Wood	Tiger
1975	Wood	Rabbit
1976	Earth	Dragon

Table 7. Chinese Signs and Elements (cont.).

YEAR OF BIRTH	ELEMENT	CHINESE ASTROLOGICAL SIGN
1977	Fire	Snake
1978	Fire	Horse
1979	Earth	Goat
1980	Metal	Monkey
1981	Metal	Rooster
1982	Earth	Dog
1983	Water	Pig
1984	Water	Rat
1985	Earth	Ox
1986	Wood	Tiger
1987	Wood	Rabbit
1988	Earth	Dragon
1989	Fire	Snake
1990	Fire	Horse
1991	Earth	Goat
1992	Metal	Monkey
1993	Metal	Rooster
1994	Earth	Dog

Table 7. Chinese Signs and Elements (cont.).

YEAR OF BIRTH	ELEMENT	CHINESE ASTROLOGICAL SIGN
1995	Water	Pig
1996	Water	Rat
1997	Earth	Ox
1998	Wood	Tiger
1999	Wood	Rabbit
2000	Earth	Dragon
2001	Fire	Snake
2002	Fire	Horse
2003	Earth	Goat
2004	Metal	Monkey
2005	Metal	Rooster
2006	Earth	Dog
2007	Water	Pig
2008	Water	Rat
2009	Earth	Ox
2010	Wood	Tiger
2011	Wood	Rabbit
2012	Earth	Dragon

Table 7. Chinese Signs and Elements (cont.).

YEAR OF BIRTH	ELEMENT	CHINESE ASTROLOGICAL SIGN
2013	Fire	Snake
2014	Fire	Horse
2015	Earth	Goat
2016	Metal	Monkey
2017	Metal	Rooster
2018	Earth	Dog
2019	Water	Pig
2020	Water	Rat
2021	Earth	Ox
2022	Wood	Tiger
2023	Wood	Rabbit
2024	Earth	Dragon
2025	Fire	Snake

The element that relates to the year of birth will indicate which years will be the best for you. For example, if you were born in 1958, your Chinese astrological sign is Dog, and your personality trait is Earth. So Earth years (1961, 1964, 1967, 1970, 1973, 1976, 1979, 1982, 1985, 1988, 1991, 1994, 1997, 2000, 2003, 2006, 2009, 2012, 2015, 2018, 2021, 2023) will be good for you. These years will see you doing well—and this would be the time to make your investment decisions and forge ahead. You would relax and take it easy during your Wood years.

Index

interior decor, 79
Keiloon, 77, 104
kitchen, 96
lamppost, 33
light fixtures, 88
living room, 94
marital bliss, 82
measles, 45
Midas touch, 56
money
  comes easily, 19
  flow of, 52
  inability to save, 15
  lending, 27
  loss of, 7, 13
mountain, 40, 45, 50
  metal-shaped, 47
  rock, 47
new year, 136
nostalgia, 95
orange, 75
paintings, 95
Personal Direction Chart, 60, 107, 116
plants, 96
portraits, 95
purple, 74, 75
red, 74, 75, 95
refrigerator, 99

road, 50
satellite dish, 40
sink, 101
skin problems, 45
souvenirs, 96
stomach ailments, 45
stove, 99
sunsets, 95
Tiger, white, 47
  placement of furniture, 80
Tong Wan, 55, 57, 60, 65
  for water, 57
traffic, 52, 54, 64
tree, opposite front door, 34
underground tunnels, 38
Wan, 37, 54, 60
water, 52, 54, 57, 58, 70, 71, 133
  flow, 52
  noisy, 54
  pipes, 38
  quality, 50
wealth, 63
white, 71, 73, 75
windows, 40
Yang, 39, 94
yellow, 74, 75
Yin, 39

About the Authors

Li Pak Tin was professionally trained at the prestigious Hong Kong Park Hawk Ming Institute of Astrological Studies, and has integrated Feng Shui, Palmistry, and the Reading of Facial Features in his work. With over twenty years of practical experience, first in Hong Kong, and then in London, Mr. Li is consulted by both business people and private clients. His recommendations, based on one's date of birth, range from advice as to the use of a particular piece of land—whether it is better as a parking lot or an apartment complex—to determining the beneficial energy in commercial buildings, private homes, schools, retail shops, etc. He has done this from photographs and from personal inspection, and his client range travels from far and wide to see him.

Helen Yeap has collaborated with Li Pak Tin on a series of books including a home study course for the Regent Academy of Fine Arts in London.